Little
Miracles

Little Miracles

A Story of Courage, Faith and Survival

ABRAHAM BICHLER

www.ivyhousebooks.com

PUBLISHED BY IVY HOUSE PUBLISHING GROUP
5122 Bur Oak Circle, Raleigh, NC 27612
United States of America
919-782-0281
www.ivyhousebooks.com

ISBN: 1-57197-404-0
Library of Congress Control Number: 2003096955

Printed in the United States of America

This book is dedicated to the blessed memories of my beloved wife, Fran; my unforgettable parents, Rebecca and Solomon; my sister Saryl, who died at the age of four in the slave labor camp in the Taiga; and to all the members of our family who perished in the Holocaust.

Acknowledgments

This work would never have reached its conclusion without the encouragement and caring help I received from my children—Barry, Sherri, and Liora—and extended family. I would like to thank my sister Beatrice Bichler Jorden for helping me to remember and clarify some of the events that we shared together so many years ago. I would especially like to express my gratitude to my sister, Iris (Chaya) Bichler Fox, and my niece, Samantha Fox Bender, for their constant help in transcribing, shaping, and producing the manuscript.

Preface

"Yes, the bitterness of death is past, and death is far sweeter than honey, but not for all nations, not for all races. There is only one people to whom death is pleasant—the people of G-d, the off-spring of the three patriarchs, Abraham, Isaac, and Jacob, who wait for death but it does not come. Not even this wish is granted them. They have been allotted a long life, so that no sorrow shall escape them.

"This is the people that is as though it had never been. Every mouth devoured it; it was scattered to the corners of the earth, plundered by all nations. Before Media toppled it, Babylon consumed it; Greece swallowed it up, Ishmael did not spew it out. Why do You make its yoke heavier; why do You multiply its misery? It has neither weapons nor strength; it can no longer bear the burden.

"Make haste, go up to my Father and say to Him: 'Your son is about to die. Will You not visit him? Speak to the earth and it will tell You how he has wandered to its limits. Its dust will inform You how it was kneaded with his blood. Go to the wilderness and see how it was drenched with his tears. The blood of Your murdered people has made the desert bring forth grain.'

"Get up, call on your G-d, gather all Your dead and say to Him: 'O Lord, You are compassionate and gracious; After all this, will You hold back? You have ravaged them, You have ridiculed them, You have paid them no heed. You have given them up to be butchered like sheep and till now you have shown them no pity . . .'"

—Haya Gaon
(939–1038)
"Sweet Death"

Introduction

I have decided to give in to the demand by so many of my students, friends, and acquaintances, Jews and non-Jews alike, and tell as much as I can remember about my life history, emphasizing the years of World War II, the Displaced Persons Camps, and the coming to America.

Many people know a little about the Holocaust, in which the Nazis and their collaborators murdered six million Jews, among them more than one million children, in the most brutal ways. There are no words in any language that can describe the brutality and bestiality of the genocide perpetrated by the German people and their helpers against the Jewish nation.

However, there are few people who know that when "Father" Stalin took hundreds of thousands of people forcibly to godforsaken places in the former Soviet Union, it was not to protect us from the Nazis; it was for slave labor, much suffering, and death. It was by G-d's grace that many of these people came out alive. In this book, I shall share with you the story of my family, which is also the story of thousands of others who were in the same places.

One

I was born in Krylov, Poland, on February 23, 1933. Krylov was a small town on the Bug River, surrounded by forests, fields, and orchards; it looked like a resort area. I do not think that Krylov had street names, because for as long as my parents were alive, I never once heard them refer to a street name when talking about Krylov. However, families were nicknamed and were always referred to by those names. Ours was the Pack, meaning a lot of luggage, because we were well-to-do, and whenever we had to run away, we had a lot of baggage. Individuals also had nicknames that pointed out their shortcomings or vocation. For example, I heard my parents say that they were going to the *bris* (circumcision) of Shloime Tzaindalach's (Solomon with Irregular Teeth) son, or that Suril de Shneidarin (Sarah the Seamstress) was getting married, or that Langer (Tall) Fyvish died.

Most of the people in town believed in devils, ghosts, and all sorts of superstitions. I remember my parents telling us that if you stepped over a growing child he would stop growing. If you entered a home through the window, you wouldn't grow. If someone was sewing an item that you were wearing, you had to chew on a piece of thread while the sewing was taking place or your common sense would be sewn together. We needed to be especially careful of certain individuals because they had the evil eye. If you became ill because of someone with the evil eye, it required getting a thread or some other small piece of garment belonging to the person with the evil eye. Then someone who specialized in removing curses would be called in. The specialist would take the thread or piece of garment that was taken from the person with the evil eye and burn it, while spitting in all directions. They believed that eventually this brought about a cure.

There were people who truly believed that devils and ghosts were walking in the streets at night. My father was convinced that there was a ghost in the attic of the house his family lived in during World War I. He was prepared to swear that everyone in the family heard someone breaking bottles in the attic. But when two of our family members went up to look in the attic, they saw no glass; instead, they saw a duck. They chased the duck and tried to catch it when it suddenly jumped into a pot. When they approached the pot, they saw only an egg. They didn't dare touch the egg for fear that this apparition would harm them.

My Uncle Isaac often used to walk very late into the night to check on the family's stores, and one night as he approached our liquor store he saw someone completely covered in white sheets standing motionless. He pulled out his gun (both my uncle and father had licenses to carry guns) and with some trepidation approached this apparition. When he got close enough, he saw that it was a woman. He asked her who she was and pulled the sheet off her. It turned out to be one of the two crazy sisters in town. She was completely naked, and he chased her home. Most of the people in our town would never have dared approach this "ghost" but would have endlessly told stories of seeing ghosts in the streets during the night.

Krylov was situated between two large cities, Hrubieszow on the Polish side and Vladimir Volinskiy (also called Ludmir) on the Ukrainian side, and my family did business in both of those areas.

Now, let me explain a little bit about *yichus*, and in particular, my family *yichus*. *Yichus* is family pride, and much more. It's lineage. *Yichus* was a family's heritage of great rabbis as well as rich and influential individuals traced as far back as possible. *Yichus* was important not only in our small town, but throughout the European Jewish community. It was *yichus* that determined one's social standing and whom one would marry. Even during times of crisis, *yichus* was important; *yichus* was everything to a family. On my father's side, the two families were the Bichlers and the Brenners. My grandmother, Tova Brenner Bichler, had two brothers, one in Zamosc and the other in Hrubieszow. My great-uncle Chaim Brenner of Zamosc was very involved in the Jewish community and earned himself the reputation as a man of wisdom and uncompromising integrity. The community entrusted him with the most prestigious position of *Bes-Din Dayan*—a judge in the religious court. His son Joshua was a criminal lawyer and later served as a judge in Tarnigrod. His level of achievement was rare for a Jewish man in prewar Poland. My great-uncle Yoshe Brenner of Hrubieszow, who was a very wealthy man, also held high positions in his community. These were very distinguished, well-to-do families, and leaders in their communities.

On my paternal grandfather's side were the Bichlers. They were also a very well-to-do and highly respected business family. My great grandfather, Zayde Levi, was involved with noblemen, and oftentimes great estates would be bought and sold in his house; other times, he would escort the sons of the noblemen to Warsaw to seal deals. As his reward, he would get sometimes one hundred acres of land and sometimes more. That was quite a large fortune in the times of the czars, and even later in Poland. Zayde Levi's brother, Simcha Bichler, was a multimillionaire. He owned brick factories, ran a textile business, and sold farming equipment. So these were two very powerful families.

On my mother's side, they were working families. My grandmother, Shifra Weintraub Kurtzwald, was a seamstress. My grandfather, Yitzhak Kurtzwald, was also from a working family. However, they had something else. They had longevity and strength on their side. My great-great-grandmother was 106 years old when she died. Her name was Chaya, which means "alive." It is told that when she didn't feel well and was in bed, she knew that she was going to die. They called in her grandchildren and great-grandchildren and everybody else to say good-bye to her, and then she turned to the wall and she went to sleep and died. This was what my mother told me. As a matter of fact, many girls in our family and other relatives' families were named Chaya because it is good luck to be named after someone who lived that long. My younger sister Chaya is named after this great-great-grandmother, and hopefully she too will live until 106 at least, if not more.

My grandpa's family was very strong. My grandpa was a bricklayer. According to what I learned from my mother, he was able to take a piece of metal and just twist it around his arm as if he were putting on *tefillin* (phylacteries) with it. And his brother, whom I never knew, was even stronger. All in all, it is not a bad combination.

My Zayde Levi I remember mostly because he would help babysit for me while my father was in his store or on the road. My father was a grain merchant in partnership with his brother Isaac. My mother took care of the grocery store we had. Also, Father, his brother, his older sister Doba, and Grandpa Dov, his father, were partners in a liquor store. For a Jew to own a liquor store was not a very easy thing. It was possible only because of Zayde Levi's connections.

During Poland's revolution, some of Zayde Levi's servants went to fight, and one of them lost a leg in a battle. As a result of that war injury, he was eligible to have a liquor license, which we used, and for which we paid him monthly. Thus, we were able to have the liquor store, where we sold bottles as well as drinks.

An interesting anecdote involving Zayde Levi is that while still under the czars, before Poland became independent, he had a number of servants, one of whom served in the last czar's army. This servant was present when one of the finger rings that the czarina wore fell on the floor. When he picked it up and tried to give it back to her, the czarina would not take it from him, and the ring became his. It was a ring that could be worn on three fingers at one time, or it could be put together and worn on one finger so that it looked like a handshake. When the servant returned, he brought this ring to Zayde Levi. Zayde Levi gave it to my father's cousin Gisha, who left Poland for America with her father and two brothers after her parents' divorce. In those days, divorce brought shame on the family within the community. Unfortunately, Cousin Gisha lost the ring in America.

Zayde Levi lost his fortune before Poland became independent. What happened was, he had lots of money, all in golden rubles (coins). At one point he was preparing to buy a number of houses in Hrubieszow. The deal was arranged, and he had to travel the next day or two to pay the money. It was difficult to carry the large amount in golden coins, so he exchanged them for paper money. When he got up on the next morning, there was a total devaluation, and his paper money was completely worthless. Thus, he lost his entire fortune. He did, however, have enough money to wallpaper his house and some other houses. He never regained the economic stature that he enjoyed before, although he was always comfortable. His brother Simcha, on the other hand, kept his golden rubles, never exchanged them for paper, and remained a millionaire.

Zayde Levi was a Hasidic Jew. *Hasidism* was a popular religious movement in Judaism in the second half of the eighteenth century. Its founder was Israel Ba'al Shem Tov (Master of a Good Name), a thirty-six-year-old man from Okop Province in Podolia, Russia. His name was abbreviated to Besht. He began by ministering to the emotional needs of Jews in his neighborhood. He soon became known far and wide as a real mystic, and people began to revere him and flock to him, hanging on to his every word. Israel's teachings may be summarized as the search for G-d, the effectiveness of prayer, joyful living, and spiritual leadership. The weakest spot in the Besht's teaching was his advocacy of spiritual leaders. Such men came to be known as *tzaddikim (tzaddik* in the singular) or "righteous men." These "righteous men" were the intermediaries between G-d and man. They held court and gave personal advice; they offered religious instruction and guidance in piety. They formed the center of people's social lives. The students of the Besht and his disciples became the *tzaddikim* or Rebbes. The followers of the Rebbes were known as Hasidim. The Rebbe was considered able to transmit his standing and ability to his son or to another male member of his family. As a result, regular dynasties of Rebbes came into being; some of them continue to exist to this day (*A History of the Jews* by Solomon Grayzel, pp. 524–528).

I remember my father telling me that Zayde Levi was a Belzer Hasid, and he would have an appropriate place at the Belzer Rebbe's table when he was rich. Zayde Levi was a very charitable man and tried to help people quite a bit. He had a large house, and he rented out the downstairs to a family with a number of children. The man was what we call a *talmid chacham*, a scholar. He lived in the house for many years and never paid rent. Not only did he not pay rent, but my grandpa and his wife, Bubbe Braindl, used to provide him and his family with food as well. Oftentimes before holidays, when Zayde Levi still had large areas of land with fields and cattle and horses, he would bring in a number of wagons filled with potatoes and place them in the marketplace in the center of town for the Jewish people, the poor people, to take so they would not go hungry. This is the type of person Zayde Levi was.

I'm sure his brother, Simcha, was also charitable, but I don't think he was known to be the same type of man as Zayde Levi. I do know that Simcha died while we were all still in Krylov, and before he was buried, the *chevrei kadisha* (the group that perform the purification of the corpse) and the rabbi stopped the burial until his family promised to donate money to repair the synagogue. Once the family promised to do that, the *chevrei kadisha* went through with the burial.

Zayde Levi did not work, and when my parents were at their businesses, he played with me. We lived across the street from him with my maternal grandparents. My Grandma Shifra, who did not work, took care of me, but Zayde Levi was the one who would play with me. He was fortunate enough to die peacefully in 1939, in Vladimir Volinskiy, where he received a proper burial and did not witness the destruction of our family and the Jewish people.

My father was a Chortkover Hasid, the same as his father, my Zayde Dov. But I do not know why they were Chortkover Hasidim rather than Belzer, like Zayde Levi. Before entering the Polish army, my father received two lucky coins from the Chortkover Rebbe. The two coins were meant to protect him and have G-d watch over him. As you read on and learn of the terrible things we survived, I think you will agree that these coins, which I have today, did a marvelous job.

In addition to his brother Isaac, Father also had three sisters. I mentioned Doba, the eldest, earlier. His two other sisters were named Mindle and Munya. My mother had two brothers, Yeshayahu and Shmeryl. I do not really remember Shmeryl well, because he died when he was only in his thirties. His death was a direct result of a terrible beating he received from fellow Jews. The story goes that Shmeryl married a very beautiful girl from Yevanich, and with the help of his wife's parents, he opened a business similar to my father's, buying and selling grain. The competitors in the town warned him to get out of the business, but he refused. One day, the competitors sent a number of Jewish hoodlums to take care of him. Shmeryl was taken into a home or a synagogue and severely beaten. He was in bed spitting blood for months in our house before he died, leaving a wife and a daughter, Tonia.

I remember our house in Krylov a little bit. We had a very big garden in the back. I remember cherry trees and plum trees, and I remember that from all the way at the back of the garden we were able to see the church. We also had a barn with a dairy cow and horses. To one side of our house, we had Jewish neighbors. And on the other side, our neighbors were a Christian family by the name of Shintovsky. All of their children, especially the daughter, who was a good friend of my mother's, spoke Yiddish as beautifully as if they were Jewish. Across the street from us was my Grandpa Dov's and Grandma Tova's house. In front of the house they had a yard that was fenced off. And right near it was Zayde Levi's house. It was a tall brick building. And nearby was the drugstore. I remember going to my mother's store. On the way, we had to go up a hill, and past the hill, not far away, was the huge Bug River. Everything seems hazy now; I really cannot remember much of the town. I even have great difficulty remembering the faces of my Grandpa Dov and my Grandma Tova because we have no photographs of them. My father's sisters and brother I know only from photographs we have, and their children, my first cousins, I do not remember at all. The only face I remember quite well is Zayde Levi's. But I do remember all of my mother's family, because we were together the entire time.

I have an older sister, Beatrice, Bracha in Hebrew, who is named after Bubbe Braindl, Zayde Levi's wife. I myself am named for two grandfathers and an uncle. My other sister's name was Saryl, and she was named after my mother's brother Shmeryl (they transliterated his name to Saryl). And finally, when we had my youngest sister, the fourth child in the family, we called her Chaya.

In our town and in our area, the Jews, the Poles, and the Ukrainians lived peacefully together. And, according to what I remember my father telling us, there was seldom any fear of pogroms or any other violence of that sort. As a matter of fact, my father told me many times that the non-Jews feared the Jews more than the Jews feared them. Jews were in business with the Ukrainians and the Poles, and it worked well. For most of the dealings, my father was on the Ukrainian side, and we rarely had any problems. They were very loyal and very honest. I always remember my father saying these things. Of course, the Bichler family always had to be careful because successful business people always had enemies. And they did have quite a number of enemies—both among the Jews and the Poles, and far less on the Ukrainian side. But all in all, my family was very well connected with the town official and with the police. When a Jew from out of town was arrested in our town for purchasing a stolen horse or cow or for something else, people would come running to Father or to other members of the Bichler family for help. Our family immediately went into action, and most of the time the Bichlers were successful in obtaining the release of their fellow Jew.

In the late 1930s, anti-Semitism was beginning to spread. I remember a particular incident when I was a young boy. I was at our store one day, and Zayde Levi was sitting just outside of the store when I saw people marching in the street shouting, "Don't buy from Jews!" It was already 1939. I remember my father was saying that the Poles were spitting at Jews. My Zayde Levi was sitting there, and they knew that if they did anything they would have a fight on their hands. Our family was large, not at all fearful, and well connected with the police and town authorities. I still remember one of the Endecja leaders . . . he was a Pole with only half of his nose and he couldn't speak clearly. That made a lasting impression on me.

In Poland at this time, radical nationalist groups unleashed a reign of terror. Students and toughs began picketing Jewish stores, threatening Poles who dared to enter. Store windows were smashed; Jewish owners were knifed, beaten, and victimized. This organized pattern of terror was taking place throughout Poland. Many attacks were against the defenseless and poorest Jews, and the slogan of the Poles was "Beat up a Jew." In my town, we also had groups who shouted, "Beat up a Jew!" and "Don't buy from a Jew!" as well as a few smashed windows. But in my town, as well as in many other towns, Jews organized self-defense groups and thus prevented more serious violence and pogroms. Father, who was in the active reserves in the Polish army, received a letter at this time stating that he did not have to report for duty. Our entire family was relieved.

In about May or June, the tension became very high. There were big problems between Poland and Germany, with the Germans demanding the Danzig Corridor and of course the Poles refusing to give in. People used to gather to listen to the radio in specific places, because very few people had their own radios. I remember going with my father to listen, but I could not understand the tension. Of course I know now what went on—these were the weeks before World War II broke out. As the month of August approached, things began happening. The Russians and the Germans were negotiating secretly, and rumors briefly began spreading. On August 23, 1939, Hitler and Stalin startled the world by signing a nonaggression agreement. No one could believe that Stalin would do a thing like that. And before they signed the agreement, we know today that Stalin made a toast to the health of the German Führer. Three days later, on August 26, the Anglo-Polish Alliance was signed, and on September 1, at 5:30 A.M., Poland was invaded by Germany. This was the beginning of World War II. In our town, there was great fear of the war and the Germans, so we decided to get out.

Two

We left most of our possessions at home and in the stores. We loaded up as much as possible on wagons and we crossed the Bug River, which later became the border between Germany and Russia. We were then on the Ukrainian side, and my immediate family and my father's family stayed together at Yaska Shugars's, a very well-to-do farmer who owned large apple and pear orchards, as well as many fields. He was someone Father knew well because he had done a lot of business with him. I remember walking around and picking up the fallen fruits under the trees. Yaska hid us in his barns. My Uncle Yeshayahu and his family and Grandpa Yitzhak and Grandma Shifra went to another farmer. We stayed there for a number of days and hoped things would cool off so that we could return home. While in the barns, we saw German tanks go by and Ukrainians welcoming them with flowers. One evening, a woman came to the farm and began probing for information from the farmer. Then she asked to stay for the night. The next morning she was gone. No one knew when or to where she had disappeared. Everyone came to the conclusion that she was a German spy, and Yaska began feeling very insecure because of our presence. He feared other farmers or German sympathizers might torch his property, so my parents, my sisters, and I moved to where my Uncle Yeshayahu and Grandpa Yitzhak were staying. That farmer was Sergey. At the same time, my father's family scattered to different farmers. All this moving was done at night for our own well-being as well as for the security of the farmers and their families. My uncle and Grandpa Yitzhak knew Sergey well, because they had built his barns and part of his house.

Sergey and his family were very nice. They made us feel welcome. I remember Sergey's son climbing walnut trees and giving us the walnuts. While we were at Sergey's, the Russians moved in and the Germans moved out. We were then under the Russian army. I remember an incident where a few Russian soldiers entered the house where we were. One of them saw the picture of the Virgin Mary on the wall and said to Sergey's mother, "Who is this prostitute?" She was beside herself; she fell to her knees and began crossing herself. The Russian soldier had no idea who he was talking about.

With the Russians, we had a feeling of security, and after a number of days, we moved back home to Krylov because the Soviets had occupied our town and we believed it was safe. When we came back to our home, we found that the Germans had been in our house. We found food left by them, and we discovered that our neighbors stole one of our doors and some windows. However, most of our furniture and other belongings remained untouched.

Many other people also returned to their homes. With the Russians in town and many people not having money, they began trading with the soldiers. All this was done in the town's market square. The soldiers bought everything, especially watches, clocks, and clothing. With the Soviets present, the town's Communists, many of them Jews, began to take over the town. On a Saturday, when my father was in the synagogue, one of our neighbors, accompanied by a number of his Communist friends, came into the sanctuary and asked for the keys to our store in order for him to take out the merchandise so he could distribute it to the needy people. My father asked if it was okay if he went with them to open the store, rather than giving them the key. They were gracious enough to accept this offer. Father went home, took the key, and opened the store, and they took out everything. They did the same thing to many of our relatives and other well-to-do people. They put the merchandise on wagons and drove around distributing to the peasants the wealth of those who worked all their lives to accumulate it. These Communists had a terrible hatred for the well-to-do.

At this time, my father's cousin Kuperman (Simcha Bichler's grandson) came home from the front line after fighting in the Polish army against the Germans. He walked from village to village after his battalion was disbanded. Those who survived were told to make their way home as best they could. After being back for a day or two, the Jewish Communists came to his home. They put on hoods, like the Ku Klux Klan in America; they took him outside, told him to open his mouth, and they put a bullet right through him. One of the people involved in the killing was the same man who came in demanding the key to my father's store. This was done because he was from a very rich family.

After about two weeks in town, the bad news was back. The Soviets were pulling out. We left before the Germans arrived. This time, we loaded up everything on wagons, and for the second time, we crossed the Bug River, which was the border between Germany and Russia. The river in our town was not guarded, but the "bridge" (a platform that moved from one side of the river to the other) was destroyed.

Crossing the river was not a very easy thing. We had loaded up the wagons with everything we had in the house; the children and the adults went across the river on horses led by a person who had great knowledge of the area, and then the wagons came through. I can still remember it. It was not a picnic, obviously. We left the house this time, never to return again.

This time, we went to my father's cousin in Pritzk. They gave us a room with a number of beds. We did not know how long we would stay, so we registered my sister in school because she always had a great will to learn. From great excitement, she did not sleep all night. Early in the morning, she went to school only to find out that the school was closed. One morning in Pritzk, it was so cold in the room that my sister's hair froze to the headboard. After about a week, we moved on to Yevanich to stay with my mother's late brother's wife and our cousin Tonia. We stayed there only three or four days, and then we moved to Vladimir Volinskiy, where all of my mother's and father's families were. We joined my mother's family, who were staying with their first cousin, Rivka (she, my mother, and another cousin were all named for the same person).

We were in Vladimir Volinskiy for about four weeks. In the beginning, our cousin thought it would only be a week or two, but as it was dragging on, she was not very pleased and became very impatient with us. All the people who came to the Ukraine were called *byezniches*, which meant refugees. At this time, people began lining up at the German offices and signing up to go back to their homes. I remember being there with my father. I can't remember whether we stood on line or were looking for familiar faces, but there were huge lines of mostly non-Jews. I did not mind living in Vladimir Volinskiy. Across from us was a soccer field. My cousin was a soccer player, and I, for the first time in my life, saw the game and loved it.

Meanwhile, my mother's cousin didn't have patience for our extended stay. Without saying anything to anyone in the family, she went to the Russian authorities and informed them that there were refugees from the other side of the river staying at her home illegally. Whether she sent someone to do it or she did it herself, we never knew, but we know she *did* inform on us. In the middle of the night, a large Russian truck drove up to the house we were in. The Russians knocked on the door, opened it, and took our family (my mother, father, my two sisters, me, my uncle and his family, my maternal grandparents, and another cousin, also named Rivka, who always traveled with us) and everything that we had and put us on that truck. My father tried to explain to them that he was born in Vladimir Volinskiy, which meant that he was a citizen there and therefore had the right to stay there, but they refused to listen. They took us with our belongings and brought us to a huge cattle train that was standing at the railroad station and shoved us in with thousands upon thousands of other people.

We stayed on that train for a number of days because it was a huge train and they tried to load it up totally. They took everything a person had. Regardless of what it was, nothing was too big or too small, including furniture. Our family in town found out about our situation and tried everything in their power to get us off the train and keep us in town. They went to the authorities and brought proof that my father was born there. It did not help; nothing helped. But somehow, they proved to the satisfaction of the authorities that they were born there. Nobody bothered them; nobody touched them. My father's parents, my father's brother and his three sisters, each one married and with children, all of my father's uncles and cousins, and Zayde Levi—they all remained there.

One of the Ukrainian peasants, I believe that it was the one that we stayed with for a week or so, somehow found out that we were on that train. It seemed he owed my father some money, so he brought us two sacks of sugar as payment. This sugar came in very handy.

While we were on the train, no one from my father's family dared to come see us off and say good-bye. They were terribly afraid that they too would be placed on this horrible train and sent off to G-d knows where. Only my Grandpa Dov rented a coach, and he rode by the train looking at us while we were waving at him. That was the last time that we saw my grandpa. We never saw him or anyone else from my father's entire family again. That evening, the train finally began moving.

Three

There were about forty or fifty people in the car, and it was very crowded. It was hot and smelly from both humans who did not bathe and animals that were previously transported in these cars. The car was divided in half, leaving room in the middle. There was an upper level and a lower level made up with planks. The upper level was better because it had a small hole for a window that provided light and air. Opposite the door was a V-shaped hole that served as the "toilet."

We were on the upper level. After traveling a little, we encircled the V-shaped hole with a blanket in order to provide some kind of privacy. After all, we were all human beings and not animals, although we were treated just like animals. People were weeping, children were crying, and the train was shaking and shaking while slowly moving into the unknown, and the unknown terrified us.

The only time the train stopped was at night, when they would open up the door of the car and bring in a huge kettle of what they called soup. It was hot water, with a few noodles inside chasing each other, and that had to be distributed to everyone in the car. I'm sure they did the same throughout the train. Nobody knew where we were going or how long we would be on this train, but we kept on going day after day after day. Sometimes we would stop. I remember once we stopped on a bridge, and somehow we managed to lower a bottle tied to a string and get a little bit of water. An old woman there said something; she was sort of blessing us and wishing for us to survive this ordeal.

The Russian soldiers kept the doors of the cars closed with a latch but not with a lock. You were able to open the door only from the outside. Maybe they feared that some might escape while we were still close to home. The heat and smell in the car was unbearable. One man in our car managed to climb out of the little window onto the roof of the car. Then he crawled to the door and somehow opened the latch. The door was opened a little so it would not be too noticeable. Fresh air came in, and everyone sucked it in. In the evening, he would crawl out and close the latch. He did this for a number of days. After a week or so, the Russians stopped closing the latch, and we were able to keep the door open.

We traveled for six weeks. The first week or so, we seldom stopped during the day, only at night. However, as time went on, we began stopping during the day, sometimes two or three times a day. Probably one of the reasons must have been that Russia had a one-rail line, and sometimes there were certain areas where you had to allow other trains to pass. Or perhaps they just wanted to give us a chance to get out. I don't know. When the train stopped, people would force the doors open from these cattle cars. Some would jump down just to get out and breathe a little bit of fresh air. Others would jump down and try to make a little fire to cook something. Some people saved the soup they were given in the middle of the night (we could never figure out why the soup was given to us in the middle of the night), and they added in a kind of farina or whatever they had with them and tried to make some kind of meal out of it. Other people went down and tried to relieve themselves beneath the train, because after all, it was just impossible in that car. The people who wanted to cook something would grab two stones and very quickly make a little fire with some pieces of wood and then put the pot on the stones and try to cook. As the people were doing what they had to do, out of nowhere the whistle would blow, and as soon as the whistle blew, without waiting even a moment, the train would start moving and people would try to get back on. Some people tried to get out from beneath the train. Others who were just out for air had no problem getting on. But those who were cooking tried to save whatever they could (the pot with the food, and sometimes the stones). Some tried to run with the pot and when they couldn't make it, they would drop the pot and everything else and try to jump aboard any car they could reach. Many times, people could not get out from beneath the train on time, and you heard terrible screams. Probably some lost their lives, and some lost their limbs. Other people just could not make it back onto the train. At times it was a person who couldn't run, and the people on the train began shouting, screaming, grabbing an arm, and pulling them into the car. Other times, they could not help; they could only watch in horror. And the conductor many times increased the speed, as if on purpose. He must have enjoyed watching this terrible tragedy. Many people lost their lives or were separated from their families, sometimes mothers, sometimes fathers, and only G-d knows whether they ever met up with their families again. I don't think my parents ever knew of anyone who met up with their family. Let's hope some did. My family only permitted my father or my uncle to go down when the train came to a stop.

The train kept on moving day and night, shaking and moving. It literally turned the people's guts upside down, and many people, especially young children, paid with their lives as a result. This misery went on for six long weeks, until we arrived to the Russian Taiga.

Four

The train finally arrived to Asina in the Taiga. The Taiga ever-
green forests of Siberia are between the northern tundra and the
southern steppes near the Arctic Circle. The railroad ended in
Asina, and the more unfortunate continued their journey by boat,
deeper into the Taiga. To us, it was the end of the earth. If there is
a such thing as hell, this was it. We were in a huge camp with tens
of thousands of people. There were Jews and non-Jews. Multitudes
of people were sitting with their bags outside waiting for something to happen. We were outside in some sort of a huge pit. After
a while people were assigned to barracks or shacks. Near where we
were sitting, a family moved out of a shack, so my father got a permit for our entire family to move in. People were running around
looking for relatives, and other people put up signs announcing, "I
am so-and-so from this town," hoping to find friends and relatives.
My father saw a sign with the name of a police officer from our
town. Asina was a very peculiar place. You were able to see the
moon and the sun at the same time. The adults were standing and
watching this phenomenon. On one side of the camp it was day-

time, while on the other side it was nighttime. Day and night changed every few hours.

We had rats the size of small cats that did not fear people at all. We feared them. We had bed bugs bigger than cockroaches. The bread they gave us, we literally soaked in water before we were able to eat it. Any other food that was given to us was full of bugs. To get hot water, we had to stand on line for hours. It was against the law to cook in the barracks, shacks, or anywhere in the camp. To cook a meal, we had to walk quite a distance outside the camp carrying the pot, food, and two bricks for the pot to cook on to a place where hundreds of other families were also cooking, and then we had to bring it back in order for the family to eat.

When we arrived to Asina, our sister Saryl was already sick. Mother decided to stop giving her solid food. She was walking among the pots, looking for something to eat. She was very hungry. In our shack we had a broken stove and a broken chimney. Somehow, Grandpa managed to fix both, and even though it was against the law to cook in the house, we used the stove only to boil water for Saryl. We soon found out the reason why the family moved out of the shack—it was infested with *wantsen* (bed bugs), and it was especially bad at night. The bed was covered with them. Meanwhile, Saryl's condition kept getting worse. Father found doctors, but they wanted to be paid with food. This was a very big problem; we had very little food for the entire family—we had some flour and a big sack of sugar—but we decided to pay. The doctors came. They could diagnose, but they had no medicine. According to the doctors, her insides completely turned upside down because of the shaking of the train for so many weeks, and in addition, she had malaria. Saryl was getting weaker and weaker. Mother began giving away her clothing in the hope that this gesture would lead to her recovery (it was one of many superstitious beliefs the Jews from our area had). After about two weeks, when all the flour was gone and all her clothing was given away, Saryl died at the age of four. I can still see her little body lying in the crib, not moving, as if she were asleep. It was over for her; she would never be hungry again. Everybody was sitting around the crib and crying.

Suddenly we had a new worry—the burial. The authorities did not permit individual burials. Wagons rode around the camp in the evening collecting the dead from the barracks, shacks, and streets for mass burials. It was decided that Grandpa would hide Saryl's little body in the big jacket he was wearing and go into the forest to bury her. We were not in an enclosed camp with guards around us. The authorities were not concerned that we would escape, because we were in the midst of forests with nowhere to go. Only Mother and Father followed Grandpa in order not to arouse the suspicion of the authorities or any other people. They went into the forest and stood at a distance while Grandpa somehow managed to dig a shallow grave, because the ground was frozen beneath and because he had to hurry so as not to be noticed. Grandpa and my parents were bothered that the grave was shallow, not because of religious reasons, but because they were fearful that animals would get to the body. They did the best they could, and as Grandpa would say, he "left Saryl in G-d's hands."

When they got back, Saryl was not with them. My sister and I did not know what to expect, but we were looking for her and missing her terribly for a long, long time. She would continue to live in our hearts and minds forever. She was such a beautiful child that people would stop to admire her, with her big blue eyes, black hair, and pretty face.

Several days after we lost Saryl, I became very sick. Father was sent to work in the forest chopping down trees, while my grandfather and uncle worked at their trade as bricklayers. One day, I went to watch Father work. As I lay there watching, I fell asleep on the cold, damp ground and woke up with a bad case of the chills. A few days later, I was diagnosed with a combination of malaria, pneumonia, and a kidney infection. Very few doctors believed that I would survive, because there was no medication at all. The doctors were available, but not the medication.

Doctors would sometimes come twice a day; they didn't mind coming because we paid them with sugar. The only thing they did, I remember, was use *bankes* (glass suction cups) on me. The *bankes* were applied by first taking a stick and winding a piece of cotton around the tip like a very long Q-tip. When alcohol was available, they dipped the cotton tip in alcohol, then they lit it and put the flame into the glass suction cup for a couple of seconds to warm it. Finally, they placed the suction cup on the person, usually on the back. They put these *bankes* on me twice a day to break the fever. There was not a spot on my body that did not have the marks of the *bankes*. They also took urine mixed with water and put it on my forehead to bring down the fever. When we ran out of sugar, my father put the *bankes* on me himself. At this time, my mother gave away my clothing in the hope that it would lead to my recovery.

My sister Beatrice was terrified at the thought that something would happen to me so soon after she lost her sister. She used to go to the government building in the center of the camp and sit on a bench and pray for me the same prayers she heard Mother pray. This bench became her personal "synagogue." She went there almost every day and sometimes twice a day. One day, when I got a little better, my sister was left to babysit me. There was soup on the stove; she asked me if I would like some, and I said yes. She gave me the soup, not realizing there was salt in it. I had been forbidden to eat salt because of my illnesses. When our parents came back and said there was salt in the soup, Beatrice almost died of fear that something would happen to me. She ran to her "synagogue" and prayed twice as much on that day. After a short while, she, too, was infected with malaria.

I thank G-d for the doctors with the *bankes*, and for the devotion of Mother, Father, Aunt Rivka, and Grandma Shifra, who were taking turns around the clock, watching over me, picking bed bugs off me, and putting compresses on me. Thanks to them and to my sister's prayers, I survived this terrible ordeal. I'm sure they tried the same for Saryl, but she just couldn't pull through.

At this time, news spread that some people whose family members were sick or with ill children who could not take the climate would be moved to camps outside of the Taiga. My uncle and my father began inquiring about leaving. It became clear that my immediate family would have no problem, since I was very ill, my sister was infected with malaria, and my father had no trade. But Grandpa and Uncle, who were master bricklayers, would not be permitted to leave. Father and Uncle went immediately into action. They found out which people were responsible for determining who could leave, and they brought them very beautiful gifts which we had from home and notes from doctors stating that the other children in the family and I would not survive unless we got out of that climate. The gifts were accepted, and our names were placed on the list. Finally, we were going to get out of that miserable hell.

Five

Within a few days, all the families on the list were summoned to appear at the station, where the cattle cars waited for us. All in all, we were about twelve hundred people, all Jews. We boarded the train, and everyone was in better spirits, even though no one knew where we would end up. We were all happy to get out of the hell called Asina. The train ride took about two weeks. We passed through large areas of Siberia and cities such as Novosibirsk, Omsk, and Tomsk, among many others. We were given some food on the train, and when the train stopped at stations, we were permitted to get off and buy things. We were treated much more humanely. Eventually, the train reached Sverdlovsk, a very large city in Siberia by the Ural Mountains. After a day in Sverdlovsk, where we purchased some goodies such as chestnuts in syrup and pine nuts, we arrived to our destination. It was a slave labor camp in the forests outside the city of Revda, in Siberia, about one hundred miles from Sverdlovsk. Siberia is the name of most of the Asian part of Russia. It is about one and two-thirds times the size of the United States. Thousands of square miles of Siberia are forested plains with few people living on them. For years, the czars and the Communists sent exiles and criminals to cold and isolated parts of Siberia, and we joined that population. The climate was generally dry and very cold. The area is famous for its long winters, when the temperatures fall lower than at the North Pole.

The camp was called "Revda Kirpichni-Zavod," or Revda Brick Factory. We arrived in the evening. There were many barracks, and our entire family of eleven people was assigned a double room in Barrack #5. In the morning, all men and single women had to report to the commandant for their work assignments, and all children from the age of six and older had to go to school. My sister Beatrice started school, but I was still too weak to walk and could not attend class.

Outside our window, we could clearly see a high mountain with steam coming out of its peak—a volcano—no more than two or three miles from our camp. No one paid much attention to it.

The camp had not only a brick factory, but also what they called the *butova*, or quarry, where they used explosives to smash huge rock formations. Those rocks were loaded onto small wagons and shipped off to be crushed and made into cement. Father, Uncle, Aunt Rivka, and many others loaded those rocks onto the wagons. It was backbreaking work, twelve hours a day. After a number of months, my father, uncle, and many others were transferred to load bricks onto rail cars. If people showed up five minutes late, they were forgiven the first time, but the second time, they were put in jail for half a year. The fear was so great that my father and the entire group of Jews who worked there made a deal with the authorities that they would load the wagons any time necessary, but not be marked late. The authorities agreed to the deal, and thus they often worked seventeen or eighteen hours a day. When the authorities needed them, they would blow a whistle, and the group of Jews would go, many times in the middle of the night. They were willing to do anything to stay out of the Russian jails.

In our camp, there were all kinds of people. Certain individuals tried to find favor in the eyes of the authorities or to receive special favors by becoming informers for the authorities. We had people who informed on families that were very rich, or what the Russians would call "bourgeois" or "capitalist." The Russians, of course, did not like the bourgeois, so they would come into those people's homes and start to search. The excuse was that they were looking for black marketeers or products bought on the black market. With one of the families in our barrack, they found a number of gold watches. That was sufficient proof that the family was bourgeois, and the head of that family was arrested. When we saw what was happening, my father, who had a beautiful gold pocket watch that he had received either for his wedding or his bar mitzvah, became afraid to hold onto it. He took the watch to the forest and buried it there for more than a year. I'm glad to say that it survived; I have it today, and it works beautifully.

A week or so after we buried this watch, they came into our home and began to search, because somebody informed on us too. And when they began searching, my grandfather was at home, and he asked them what they were looking for. Their answer was illegal foods that we bought on the black market, and he said to them, "You are looking in the pockets of suits and pants for illegal food?" They looked at him, told him to shut up, and continued ripping off the pockets from the suits. They looked and looked and couldn't find anything, so they finally left. We were very fortunate, and very happy.

In Siberia, the winters are very, very harsh. There, you do not measure snow in inches, but in feet. In 1940, it began snowing before Rosh Hashana. The men were told to chop wood and prepare for winter. My father and uncle chopped as much wood as possible. Most of the room we lived in was covered with wood. If you did not prepare, you could not go to the forest to chop more wood; it was prohibited. Occasionally, Father or Uncle would steal some small logs of wood that were piled up near the railroad tracks. When a search for missing wood was expected, the logs were hidden in bed with the children. Wood was a luxury, and we had to use it sparingly.

Officially, no holidays or religious observances were permitted, so everyone worked on Rosh Hashana and on Yom Kippur. Those who did not work, like my grandpa, prayed quietly at home. No organized services were permitted. On Yom Kippur, my father and uncle were working while fasting all day. The only observance I remember was on Chanukah, the Festival of Lights, when Grandpa cut a potato in half, made little holes in each half, put a tiny bit of oil in the holes with a little piece of cotton, and lit them while reciting the blessings. Each night, he added another half of a potato. It was a very white Chanukah.

The cold was unbelievable. Every part of people's bodies had to be covered, and any part open to the elements would freeze off. In the winter, people who worked were not provided with the special boots that the Russians had, called *valenkes*, made of very thick wool, water resistant, and warm. However, necessity being the mother of all inventions, my father and the others came up with their own innovation. Father had no socks. He put rags on his feet, put on the shoes, then put more rags around the shoes and poured water on the outside rags. The rags froze and insulated against the cold. This was the way he and others managed to survive and keep on working.

Going to school in the winter was a great challenge. The cold was so intense that all the little hairs on people's faces froze. My sister, being a very good student, was rewarded with a pair of *valenkes*. However, she had a coat that was too small on her. Nonetheless, that was the only one available, and she had to wear it. She had no gloves, and her books were hanging in a bag on her back. The drifts of snow were very high, and the kids used to slide on their bottoms instead of walking. They always walked in groups, with the bigger kids watching out for the smaller ones.

By the time my sister and the other children got to school, they were almost frozen, but it was nice and warm in school. The teacher was kind, and she used to stick the children's hands under water to unfreeze them. School did not close because of inclement weather. In school, they taught the students about nationalism and love of the USSR, the liberator of the oppressed. They were taught beautiful nationalistic songs. My sister loved to sing these songs, regardless of where she was. After a while, she started singing them in her sleep. I was able to get *valenkes* because of my ill health, but I began attending kindergarten only in the last three or four months of the school year.

Many locals used special snowshoes, especially if they were walking long distances. When the well was frozen and the snow high, Grandpa would bring snow into the room and melt it down on the stove for water. When he came back in after a few minutes, his beard was full of icicles. Literally, if you walked out and spit, the spit turned to ice before it hit the ground.

In the beginning of winter, Mother slipped and fell near the well as a result of the ice. She developed water in her knee and suffered for many, many years. After the snow melted, the authorities provided a carriage to take her to a hospital in Revda for treatments twice a month, but they did not help. I remember this well because every once in a while, I would be able to go with Mother in the horse-drawn carriage.

The very long, cold winter finally came to an end. The snow melted partially, and the sun was warm. All the women and children sat outside in their coats and warmed themselves. When the snow was all gone and spring was in the air, we were encouraged to plant gardens. First some trees were chopped down. Then, of course, we were encouraged to take out the roots for firewood, and then we had land for planting. Each barrack had its area, and every family was given a small parcel of land. Grandma and Grandpa were very good at gardening. We planted potatoes and eventually harvested bushels of potatoes from the virgin soil.

Next to us, we had a town, but you couldn't just go there any time you wanted. You had to obtain permission to leave camp to go into Revda. I remember people saying that there were some Jews living there, and we knew of a Jewish lawyer who lived in town. Even if you got permission, it didn't help, because everybody worked all day except for women with little children. Sometimes the older kids would go to town without the knowledge of the authorities. On the outskirts of town were small farms. These farmers, especially women, would sell milk, cheese, butter, and sometimes eggs. They would come around in the morning and shout, "*Malako nada? Malako nada?*" ("Do you need milk? Do you need milk?"). We would sometimes buy milk or a piece of cheese, not with money, but by exchanging things like articles of clothing or jewelry. We even exchanged Mother's wedding ring. Fortunately, we had quite a number of things, and we were able to manage better than others. We were also fortunate in the sense that we began receiving packages from my father's family in Vladimir Volinskiy. There wasn't a week that we did not receive a package or two with food and clothing. But we were eleven people. My parents shared everything with my grandparents and my uncle's family as if we were one family.

In the summer, we also managed to get certain things from the forest. We would go out to pick all kinds of berries and mushrooms and add some to our diet. With mushrooms, we had to be very careful because some were poisonous, so we took only the ones we were very sure of. We saw what happened to a family in our barrack who picked and ate the poisonous mushrooms. The entire family became violently ill; everyone thought they would die. They were all swollen and bedridden for days. My mother and sister used to visit them. They eventually recovered.

My father was a very heavy smoker, and tobacco in Russia was a luxury. He just could not do without it, and I don't think anyone ever sent us tobacco—it must have been against the law. So the Russians had a deal: if you picked a certain amount of berries (I don't remember how much, but it was a large amount) and turned them in, they would give you a package of tobacco. Then, of course, Father would take a piece of newspaper, put tobacco into it, and make a cigarette. This kept my father going. It wasn't easy, but to him, the tobacco was more important than food—he couldn't exist without it.

He missed his entire family very, very much. Father thought of them every moment of every day, and the hope of eventually reuniting with them kept him alive and going. Often, at night, he would lie down facing the wall and cry. He was always very sad.

I remember that the most berries were at the foot of the volcano mountain. We used to gather berries for hours. Being that I was very fragile, I was allowed to eat all the berries I found, and mother even added some to my pile. But no one else ate what they picked—everyone else's berries were for the tobacco. Once we went to a different part of the forest looking for berries and mushrooms, and we were lost for hours. We were terrified. You never knew what wild beast you would encounter. We continuously walked in circles and got deeper and deeper into the forest. We feared that evening would approach. Finally, we found the railroad tracks that led us back to camp. It was a great relief.

Our camp, from the point of view of a child, was not a bad place. Mountains and forests surrounded us. We roamed around freely. We would put pieces of wire or nails on the rail tracks, watch the train flatten them, insert them into pieces of wood, and make knives. In our barrack, we had the *krasni ugolog*, a party room or recreation room for socializing. Many evenings, after a hard day's work, young Russians would come with harmonicas, accordions, or balalaikas and start playing, singing, and dancing. They encouraged people to join in. Many did, and others just watched, clapped their hands, and forgot their troubles for a while. Besides, you were expected to come and socialize. Those who did not come were considered uncooperative, and everyone was afraid of the consequences. Often, the commandant came to check and see who was there.

Everyone admired the Russians with the balalaikas, their stamina and love for life. We were certain that many of them did not have much more than we had. Their future was not much brighter than ours. Yet they were full of life. They lived for the day and did not worry about the next day. We, as soon as we walked out of the *krasni ugolog*, wondered what the next day would bring.

After a while, people turned to a little humor. They began making fun of themselves. Every day, we had potatoes for breakfast, potatoes for lunch, and potatoes for supper, like the Yiddish folk song that went, "Sunday, potatoes; Monday, potatoes; . . . every day potatoes; and Shabbos, something new, a potato keugel." But only later did we appreciate those potatoes, because it could have been—and later was—much, much worse. Truthfully, the authorities kept us alive in camp mostly with potatoes. We received very little bread and sometimes a little sugar or oil. We were only hungry the last three months in camp, when there was a shortage of potatoes.

Six

Passover 1941 in Siberia was not a holiday that too many people were able to observe. We received a number of packages with matza from my father's family to make sure that we would be able to observe the holiday, but my father and grandfather felt that it would not be proper for us to have matza for eight days while so many other orthodox people would not even have a single matza for the Seder. Father and Grandpa distributed our matza to the orthodox families in our barrack so that they too could have a Seder, and we were left with enough matza for the first two nights of Passover. The other families were very thankful. To them, it was almost like manna from Heaven, because they would be able to fulfill the commandment to eat matza on Passover. They blessed us many times over for this deed.

The Seder in Siberia in a slave labor camp was not a celebration of joy and freedom. On the contrary, we saw ourselves as our forefathers in Egypt. They were slaves to Pharaoh, and we were slaves to Stalin and the Communists. They waited for redemption and freedom, and so did we. G-d heard their outcry and sent

Moses; our outcry had not yet been heard. We were still waiting for our Moses. We felt that we could write our own Haggadah.

Father, Uncle, and Aunt Rivka came home from a hard day's work. They washed, and we sat down to the Seder. Mother and Grandma lit little candles. We did not always have candles—many times, Mother and Grandma would say the blessing over burning matches—but the blessing had to be said. Grandpa made Kiddush over a glass of tea; we had no wine. We had prayer books, but no Haggadah. The kids asked the four questions, and Grandpa said the prayers either from the prayer book or from memory. We ate matza, potato soup, and potato keugel. Then we said the Grace After Meals. We could have bought a chicken for the holiday from the women who sold milk, but we did not because there was no *shochet* (ritual slaughterer) in our camp. We did not touch meat for the entire period in Siberia. Others did buy chicken and chopped off their heads; we were vegetarians. It was a short Seder; you never wanted the authorities to know, see, or hear what was happening in your room. After the Seder, my parents reminisced about Passovers with Father's family at home. Father said that this year his family's holiday was ruined because we were not with them.

Weeks after Passover, the snow was gone, the trees began budding, and the terrible cold winter was over. Everything came back to life. By then, I was fully recovered and finally felt like all other normal children. I began to attend kindergarten. In camp, food was getting scarcer, and again we began going to the forest to supplement our diet. My family began selling more clothing and jewelry for food and money. Nobody complained about having potatoes three times a day—we wished we had more of them. We kept going to the *krasni ugolog*. These were indoctrination meetings the adults attended to learn about the greatness of communism and the freedom-loving government of the USSR.

Meanwhile, we received letters from Father's family in Vladimir Volinskiy informing us of their move to Kremenets, about one hundred miles deeper into Soviet territory. Father could not understand why they would leave an area where, for generations, we had business connections with so many farmers and peasants. He never learned the reason, because we lost all communication with our relatives.

As of June 22, 1941, when Hitler startled the world again by sending the Nazi war machine across the Soviet border, we never heard from our family again. With the outbreak of the war, things got much worse: less and less food, very few potatoes, lots of onions, no packages from our family, and worst of all, no communication from them. Father walked around very sad and helpless. We had no radio or newspapers to know what was really happening. The only news we had was what the indoctrinators told us: that the Red Army was occupying strategic points. We felt that they were not telling us the entire story, otherwise we would have heard from our relatives, who lived more than one hundred miles away from the Bug River, which, at that time, was the border with Germany.

One summer day, all men were called to a meeting. They were told that as part of a pact made on July 30, 1941, between the Soviet Union and the exiled government of Poland in London, the Soviet Union was granting amnesty "to all Polish citizens now detained in Soviet territory either as prisoners of war or on other sufficient grounds. . . ." The amnesty was given at the joint request of the Polish government and the government of Great Britain, the ally of the USSR in the war against the Germans. What it meant was that we were free to leave the slave labor camp in Siberia and go to other areas in the USSR. Within a day or two, the man with the gold watches who was arrested for being a bourgeois, and therefore an enemy of the state, was released from jail.

I remember going to see him with my father. He was a broken man, lying in bed, white as a sheet, and speechless. In camp, people held meetings deciding what to do.

My family and a large group of other families decided that we should go to a warm climate. Originally, we wanted to go to the Crimea, but the Germans cut the railroad lines, so we opted for central Asia, where the climate is the opposite of Siberia. The authorities agreed to permit us to charter seven cattle cars for which the families would have to pay a certain amount of money (it was not much), and we would be transported to central Asia. We tried to save some food for the journey, but it was not easy. My sister, with a number of other children, went to the town hoping to be able to buy a little food with money, but there was none to buy.

Seven

The day finally came when we boarded the train for our journey. Most of our possessions were in a crate that many times doubled as a piece of furniture. We knew that we were going to central Asia, but to many of us, central Asia was nothing more than a geographic location. It was a vast area with such republics as Uzbekistan, Kazakhstan, Tajikistan, among many others. But to where in central Asia we were going, we did not know. Our only thought was to get out of where we were.

Our cattle cars were attached to a large transport, and we were on our way. When we came to Svedlovsk, our cars were attached to a different transport. They kept attaching and detaching our cattle cars from transport to transport. Many times, we waited a day or two before we were connected to another transport. Our journey lasted several weeks. It was not easy; food was very scarce because we brought along very little. We had to be very stingy with the little money that we had. We managed to exchange a number of clothing articles for food. It was very difficult, but we survived.

We finally arrived to Alma-Ata, the capital of Kazakhstan, near China. We were ordered off the train, onto a large lot near the station. The lot had some trees on one side and empty houses on the other side, but we were not permitted to move in. In the back of the houses were porches, and some fortunate people ended up on a porch with their families. The not so fortunate were under trees or on the open lot. We were under a tree. There were no facilities except running water from a pipe. For toilets, you had to go to the station. I remember seeing people urinating all over the place. One incident stuck in my mind. I remember watching a woman feed her young child and saying to him, "Look, look, look," pointing to his father urinating on a wheel of a broken wagon while she pushed a spoonful of food into the child's mouth. The circumstances were terribly degrading.

After a number of days in Alma-Ata, the men went to the authorities inquiring about work and settling in the city. The authorities did not permit us to remain in Alma-Ata, so we moved on, but in smaller groups, usually with families from the same town or with families we had gotten to know well. We had to find a place that we could call home until the war was over. Our group managed to get on a train (all of the trains we used were cattle cars) heading in the direction of Tashkent, Uzbekistan. The train took us through areas of Kirghizia, and finally we reached the city of Chimkent in Kazakhstan. It was very close to Tashkent.

Tashkent had a large Jewish population. During the 1920s and 1930s, Tashkent became one of the centers to which active members of the Zionist organization and members of the pioneering youth movement were exiled. In general, Uzbekistan in 1941 had many more Jews than Kazakhstan. There were two communities of Jews in Uzbekistan. The ancient one consisted of the Jews of Bukhara, who according to their tradition, emigrated from Persia at the time of the persecution of King Peroz (A.D. 458-485), and some considered themselves descendants of the exiles of Samaria. The second community, the new one, was of eastern European origin. Tashkent became one of the most important absorption centers for refugees from the German-occupied regions.

In Chimkent, we stayed on porches of houses near the station for two days. As in Alma-Ata, the authorities would not permit us to remain. Knowing that there was no hope of entering Tashkent, we decided to move on. We boarded a train going deeper into Kazakhstan but still not far from Uzbekistan. After a day or two, we were ordered off the train and found ourselves in the middle of nowhere. It was a godforsaken little station with nothing but sand all around us. All these families with kids and elderly were running around not knowing what to do.

After a short time, we found out that we were between the cities of Turkestan and Kzyl-Orda. With little choice, the men got together and decided to look around and determine where would be the best place to go. Some men jumped on a train going to Kzyl-Orda and others toward Turkestan, which was much closer. Some men remained to look after their families. It was almost like a spy mission. My father and uncle went to Turkestan. They decided it was not a bad place, from what they were able to see. They came back the same day. The train that they took on the return trip did not have a scheduled stop in the little station where we were, so with no choice, my father and the other men paid the conductor a small amount of money so he would slow the train down enough for them to jump off. The conductor slowed the train down, but not much. In the beginning, when some men saw their families, they jumped, and some got hurt badly. A bit later, the conductor slowed down some more and the rest of the people jumped off safely.

We, and a number of the other families, decided to go to Turkestan. The rest went to Kzyl-Orda. Fortunately, the next morning, a train going toward Turkestan stopped at the little station. We boarded the train with the other families, and we all hoped for the best. When we got off the train, we discovered that Turkestan was divided into two parts. One was the area around the train station, and about six kilometers further was the city.

As we tried to decide where to settle, a number of trucks appeared. They put all our belongings on the trucks and took us away, not telling us where or why. After about an hour or two, the trucks slowed down, kicking up a lot of dust, and stopped at a house. They unloaded the trucks, and we were in the middle of a *kolkhoz*, a government-owned and planned collective farm. We saw nothing around us except brown dusty fields. A man was there to welcome us, but we did not pay attention to him.

The women and children began crying that we would perish in this wilderness; the men began shouting that we wanted to go back. The trucks slowly began moving and kicking up dust, and all the people grabbed the bags while the women and children cried and followed the trucks in the dust. We walked about one kilometer before the trucks stopped, backed up, loaded everything on the trucks, and took us back to the station. As soon as we got back, all the families decided to settle by the station and not go into the city. My father and uncle ran around all over town looking for a place to stay, because we feared remaining at the station.

By evening, Father and Uncle rented two rooms for our family of eleven people and at the same time, managed to register at the government office for work. Everyone took a bundle, Father and Uncle moved the crate, and we moved into the house on Rovna Street. The rooms were small, with very little furniture. The house, or *kibidka* as the locals called it, was made of mud. The cooking was done on the outside. There was a small courtyard with a wall around the property. At the side of the courtyard was a place with a hole in the ground with just two walls that served as a toilet for all the families in the courtyard. The owner of the property was an Uzbek, whom everyone called Babai. He was constantly sitting on a little rug with a string of beads in his hand, near a samovar and a *narghileh* (a water pipe), drinking hot tea and smoking in front of his door. He was one of the religious leaders in town. The Babai's house was across from us. It was quite nice inside. When the door was open, we could see a large room with a floor covered with rugs. On the side of the room was a pile of small rugs, and in the middle was a very low table, with no chairs or other furniture. Next to the door, near the samovar, was his donkey, with all the dung and stink, as well as a huge, gentle dog. Next door to us, in two different *kibidkas*, were two additional families. One was a Jewish woman with two children, Celina and Kubush. The woman was their aunt, not their mother. Their mother had died, and she was their mother's sister. The father was very rich and lived in Australia. He supported them by sending them money while at the same time working with the government on getting them out of Russia to Australia. The father had no idea that his wife was dead because the aunt communicated with him as if she were the wife. After several months, they disappeared, without anyone knowing where or why. We believed she was afraid that someone would kidnap the children and thus moved from place to place. While at the Babai's, Celina and Kubush never attended school.

The other family, non-Jewish, were also refugees from the German-occupied region of Russia. There was a mother with two small boys—Misha, who was my age, and his younger brother. Their father was at the front, fighting the Germans.

Turkestan had a community of Bukhara Jews, as well as eastern European Jews from the occupied regions of the USSR. Most of the Bukhara Jews lived in the city. There was also a Jewish cemetery in the desert area between the station and the city. As we settled in at the Babai's, Grandpa and a number of other elderly Polish Jews made contact with Bukhara Jews. Grandpa's group, with the help of a Bukhara Jew named Aaron, who must have been a leader in the community, opened a small synagogue. Aaron provided the Torah scroll. It was said that the scroll was buried in the Jewish cemetery for many years. The authorities did not like the idea. The group claimed that they were Polish citizens and needed the synagogue, as well as the right to use the cemetery. The authorities gave in, but they kept an eye on who was going into and coming out of the synagogue. Grandpa's group also set up the burial society for purification of the corpse, in accordance with Jewish law, before burial. All these undertakings were done with the help and guidance of Aaron. I remember him well; he often came to see Grandpa.

Life in Turkestan was very primitive among the locals. It reminded us of the prayer to "renew our days as of old." It was almost as if we were living in the days of the Bible. Their garments were similar to what we are accustomed to seeing in movies portraying biblical life, and so was their behavior. The men, regardless of where they went, carried large staffs on their backs, with their hands wrapped around them. The married women covered their faces with veils.

There were very few bathrooms. It was commonplace to see women or men walk to the side of the street, sit down, relieve themselves with these big garments covering them, use a stone or a leaf, when available, to clean themselves, and walk away. There was no hesitation; nobody felt any shame. We also saw women walking around with rings going through the middle of their noses, and we wondered how they would clean their noses after sneezing, or even wipe their noses. But obviously, they had no problem. In their society cleanliness was not very close to godliness. When they ate, they used their fingers as flatware. And they were very efficient at it. They had ovens outside where they baked their *lipyoshki*, very large pita bread. They put on a glove like a baseball mitt, put the dough on the glove, and stuck it to the roof of the oven. For firewood, they used the dried-up droppings of camels, which looked like disks. Their main food was rice, cooked in the fats from the *kurduk* of the sheep. (Their sheep were very fat, with behinds so big that many times, they had to be supported by little wheels in order to move around. These behinds were called *kurduks*.)

Thick walls surrounded all the locals' properties. The width of these walls was about a foot or more, and many locals used them as if they were sidewalks, walking from place to place. They hated the Russians because they were nonbelievers, and of course, they did not particularly care for any other Europeans, either. Only the young ones spoke the Russian language; the elders did not, and they didn't care. They never made an effort to speak it. The young ones went to their own school. I remember the school that I went to had mostly European children; very few were Uzbeks. They would also get their religious training in their schools. They were not very patriotic. I remember whenever we saw a Russian unit march through, they always marched very smartly, until the end of the unit, where there were a few Uzbeks who were always out of step. I think they did it on purpose. The Uzbeks wanted to show how bad they were so they would be excused from the army. We heard stories that some of them would shoot off their toes in order to be excused from the army. It was also common among them for the women to do the work while the men just sat around.

We continued living at the Babai's, and times got worse. The hunger began to creep in slowly but surely. Father, especially, worked very hard. Just as the primitive lifestyles of the Uzbeks and Kazaks reminded us of the Bible, so did my father's work. My uncle was a master builder, but my father, not having a trade, had to do backbreaking menial work. He and a few others would dig a huge pit, put dirt, water and straw into it, roll up their pants as high as possible, go into the pit, and for hours, knead and knead this mixture until it became mortar. Then they would take a form made of wood, like a small rectangular box with two handles on opposite sides, fill the mortar into the form, take a little water to smooth out the top, then pull the form out, and the mortar would remain in the shape of a brick. They would make thousands of these bricks, day in and day out. Complete fields of bricks would be baking or drying in the sun, where the temperatures reached as high as 120°F–130°F. It was extremely hot, but not humid; it was desert climate. My father, in the pit, and my uncle, in the building, were working from morning until evening. It brought to mind the Passover Haggadah: "They made the Jews' lives bitter with hard service, with mortar and bricks, and with all manner of service in the field." This work went on for over a year. When the foreman saw the great work my uncle and his team did, he moved the whole team to do work in more important places. The next place of work for Uncle and Father was at a small airport near us where they were training pilots. They had to do some building in the *stolova*, the restaurant for the pilots. I remember it very well.

I used to visit them so that I would get something to eat. In that restaurant, they permitted me to come in after the pilots finished eating, and if they left something over, I was allowed to eat it. I remember coming in one time and finding some leftover meat. Boy, oh boy, did I enjoy it! I recall cutting a piece of meat to taste it, and I chewed, and chewed, and chewed, and nothing happened. It was like chewing on a piece of rubber. So I cut smaller pieces and just swallowed them, because chewing did not help. I found out later it was camel meat. I don't know if all camel meat is this way or if this was just an old camel, but be that as it may, I thought it tasted great. Anything to fill the stomach. At this point in time, there was starvation all around us throughout the area.

The man in charge of my father was an officer in the army. One night we were sleeping and suddenly, we heard a knock at the door. It was the officer coming to tell Father and Uncle where they should go to work next. My father put his pants on and let the officer in. When the officer left, we heard a shot. Before my father had a chance to take off his pants there was another knock on the door. We opened the door, and the police were there. It seems that one of the neighbors who worked for the government had a gun and saw the officer enter and leave our house. Because the officer was out of uniform, our neighbor thought he was a robber and fired at him when he came out, and the officer returned fire. Since he was seen coming from our house, the police came to us. To complicate matters more, when the police saw my father still in his pants when he should have been asleep, they immediately took it to mean that my father had just run into the house and was probably the thief. As a result, they arrested my father. It took a day or two until my uncle managed to track down the officer and get him to testify that it was he who came to the house concerning their work, that it was he who returned fire, that my father was not involved, and that there was no thief. It was only after that testimony that they let my father go. How fortunate we were, because a few days later, this officer was shipped out with an army unit to the front. If we had not found him then, my father would never have come out of that jail. In the Soviet Union, you were guilty until proven innocent. We could not help but think of those special coins the Rebbe gave to my father to protect him and to have G-d watch over him . . . .

By this time, hunger and disease were all around us. The two Russian boys with the big dog, who lived next door to us and played together with me, were so hungry that they bit the tips of their fingers off. We all suffered hunger, but we had a little more than they did. Many times, I would share with them whatever I had. We used to go around together looking to pick up anything we thought we could eat. We just wanted to have something to put in our mouths—something to swallow. We drank water and walked around with big swollen bellies. The Babai and his family did not suffer from hunger, but never did they give any of us something to eat.

By this time, typhus and other diseases were widespread. It hit our family very hard. First, my uncle's youngest daughter Gucci was hit by a disease causing blindness. It affected many children, and we were all inoculated against the disease by the authorities. But for Gucci it was too late. She also suffered from malnutrition and eventually typhus. She finally died at the age of two. Within two or three months after Gucci's death, her mother, Faige, Uncle's wife, died. We did not even know of what disease. She was only in her mid-twenties.

A number of weeks after Uncle lost his wife, he was walking in the street with his boyhood friend Shaye, Shimon Chashles (Son of Simon the Lumberjack). My sister Beatrice was very curious to know where they were going and began to follow them. Suddenly, a number of local thugs began making fun of them and shouting, "*Karak, karak!*" ("Thief, thief!"). Uncle and his friend knew they were in trouble and started running. Within minutes, there were dozens of locals yelling, "*Karak, karak*," throwing stones, and chasing after them. They caught up and began beating them. Uncle was beaten mostly on the temples. His face was full of blood. My sister ran behind Uncle, telling him, "Run home, run home!" They finally reached Shaya's house. By then, there was a mob. Someone in the house opened the door and grabbed Shaye inside, while outside they kept beating Uncle. Beatrice ran between the thugs, jumping on those who were beating Uncle. She acted so spontaneously that she did not realize what she was doing. Somehow, they stopped beating him and began focusing on the house. She yelled to Uncle to run home. He replied, "I don't know how to get home." He was totally confused. She told him to follow her. Beatrice finally brought him home. By this time, her soles were full of blisters from running barefoot for such a long time on the hot sand. We closed the door and windows and began tending to Uncle. As soon as Grandma saw Uncle, she fainted. It took a long time for Uncle to get better. He was afraid to leave the house for fear that he might be recognized, but after a number of weeks things got back to normal.

It did not take long for all the Jews to learn that the biggest mistake one could make was to show a sign of weakness and run away when the locals started up with us. If we stood our ground, hit back hard enough, they respected us and left us alone. That is precisely what happened many times after my uncle's beating.

Eight

We lived at the Babai's for over a year. Then, as my father and uncle made more connections and were able to get better jobs in more responsible places, my uncle and father found out that there was an abandoned little house that consisted of a large room, a small room with a wooden floor, and an attached barn with a collapsed roof. The authorities, because they liked my uncle and my father, permitted us to move into this house. We were very happy about the move. The new address was Pyervamiskaya 5, which means First of May Street, #5. That was an important move. There was a huge courtyard with beautiful houses, and numerous distinguished people lived in them. Amongst the VIPs was the head of the NKVD (KGB). His name was Yogoda. He lived there with his wife and two sons, one of whom was my age and one who was about two years younger. Next to Yogoda were his sister Lisa and her husband, who was in charge of the Rai Patreb Sayuz, the place that distributed food products to the stores. They had a son named Fema. We had a Christian family by the name of Koslov, who lived in a separate house, closer to us. They were quite well-to-do. They were at one time very rich, and Stalin had exiled them to this place years before World War II broke out. We also had a few other neighbors, both Jewish and non-Jewish. It was a large yard of more than two acres. Our little house was all the way at the end, touching the wall that went around the complex, and it was the only one made of mud and with no electricity. When we got there, we could not use the other people's facilities. I remember that we dug a water well for our needs. We also made a toilet with total privacy for ourselves. By this time, my father and uncle were moved to the *zagot-zerno*, the grain silos, to build something. The move we made did not change our situation much at the beginning. We were still hungry. The authorities issued every individual a bread card. This card entitled each of us to three hundred grams of bread a day and about five hundred grams for each working person. To get the bread, we had to get on line many hours before the store opened, and sometimes we would get on line in the evening for the following morning. We wanted to make sure that when we reached the window, they would still have a piece of bread for us. Standing on line was a learning experience. We were on line with Jews, Russians, Uzbeks, Kazaks, Tatars, and others. The strangest people were the young Uzbek girls. They all had long hair, and they used to search for lice in each other's hair. When they found one, they put it into their mouths, squeezed it between their front teeth, and spit it out. They found lots of them, and it turned our stomachs to watch, but we got used to it. (In Russia, they had a saying: *"Previknesh ne previknesh zdochnesh"*—"You will get used to it; if not, you will drop dead.") They explained that it was their way of getting their blood back from the lice. When we finally got to the window, we received a piece of soggy bread. The bread allowance was on a gram basis, and those in charge of its distribution used to saturate the bread in water to make it heavier. A dry three-hundred-gram slice is bigger than a wet three-hundred-gram slice. Therefore, if their job was to distribute the equivalent of 3,000 pounds of bread, with a bit of water, it easily became 3,100 pounds. Once they distributed the three thousand pounds, they closed the store, and the rest of the bread was stolen and sold on the black market. In Russia, everyone had to steal in order to survive. That was common; it was expected, and if you worked in a place where you could steal, you were fortunate. If you worked in a place where you couldn't steal, then you suffered.

Once my father and uncle began working in the *zagot-zerno* and we were hungry, they tried to steal a little wheat. How did they steal a little wheat? Father would wear heavy, ankle-high shoes—somehow he managed to get hold of such shoes. He used to put a little bit of wheat into each shoe, wrap a rag around his foot, and put his foot into the shoe. We had no socks. For hours, he walked around with the wheat in his shoes. When the day was over, the workers would line up for the guards to search them in case they were carrying out any wheat. The guards seldom looked in the shoes, because how much could you take in a shoe? Uncle did the same as Father, and at home, we would wash the wheat a number of times. It did not take long in that hot sun to dry it for the following day. We borrowed grindstones to use as a hand mill. We laid one flat stone on the bottom and a heavy circular stone on the top. The circular stone had two holes—one in the middle and one on the side. The hole in the middle was for adding grain, and the hole on the side was where we held a stick to enable us to turn it round and round and round. We did this until we made flour out of the wheat. It was not easy. It was like reliving the days of the Bible where these stones were called *richaim*. We used this flour to make bread and other food. Many times, after eating it, some of our family members would vomit, perhaps because it was full of sweat and washing it did not help much. But it did not stop us from looking forward to eating it again. After a while, Father invented another way of stealing a bit of wheat. He took along a small sack into which about a pound of wheat would fit. When no one watched, he would fill it up and hide it. After school, I would go over to play in the sand outside the back wall of the *zagot-zerno* and wait. I knew more or less the direction where he worked. At the first opportunity, Father would throw the sack over the wall. When I saw the little bag, I would look around first to see that nobody saw me. If I saw a person walk, I just played and ignored the bag, as if I hadn't seen anything. Only when it was clear did I grab it and take off very, very quickly, making sure that nobody saw and nobody followed. It was survival of the fittest. We did this quite a number of times, but never more than once a day.

For some, it was survival. For others, stealing was to get rich. The wheat at the *zagot-zerno* was supposed to be for the people in bad times, and the times could not have been any worse than they were. Yet the wheat was not distributed; it was stolen by a few people. I remember the face but not the name of the man in charge of the *zagot-zerno*. He was a tall, heavyset fellow. He and his assistants made a deal with the workers handling the wheat—the workers could carry out as much wheat as they were able for large sums of money. How did they carry out the wheat? They would come to work with two pairs of pants on. The bottoms of the pants were tied with a rope. Before leaving, they would stuff as much wheat as could fit between the two pairs of pants, and in this way, they carried out vast amounts of wheat over time.

Many times, I would go to wait for my father and uncle to come out. I would stand perhaps ten feet away from the gate, and I would see the workers who were carrying out wheat walking like wooden soldiers. They could not bend. Of course, there were guards, but these guards were part of the scheme. This went on for many months. Because some people wanted to get rich quickly, countless children whose fathers were giving their lives on the front lines were walking around half swollen, biting their fingers and dying of hunger. Eventually, after about two or three years, these people were caught and brought to justice. I remember going to the trial every once in a while with my father. To him, it was very interesting because he knew the people, and that was where I saw the head of the *zagot-zerno*. They were all convicted. The head was sentenced to fifteen years in jail, the others to lesser terms. Nobody believed that the punishment fit the crime; they should have received a punishment more like Haman's* punishment, at least the head of the *zagot-zerno*. But he most probably paid the judges off.

After about six months in the *zagot-zerno*, my father and uncle were moved to the Rai Patreb-Sayuz, a place that distributed food products to the stores. The man in charge was our neighbor in the complex, Mr. Kagan, who was Yogoda's brother-in-law.

Unfortunately, the Rai Patreb-Sayuz did not distribute every-thing they received. A lot was stolen and sold on the black market. We began to live a little bit better because the Kagans trusted us. They didn't fear us as they feared others. Many times, they came to us saying, "Can you get rid of this type of food for us quickly?" Of course we could get rid of it. We would take it to the market or directly to other people, sell it, and give them the money. In this process, we too would get something. We also began to buy a sheep every once in a while. We had a *shochet* who would come into our collapsed barn and slaughter it. Then a butcher from our town would clean it and cut it up into portions, and we would sell it. Our best customers were the distinguished families who lived in our court. The profit for us was a few pounds of meat.

When I saw a *shochet* slaughter an animal, it did not bother me most of the time. But when I saw an elderly man, a father of one of

---

* Haman is the villain in the biblical book of Esther. Everyone bowed to Haman except Mordecai the Jew. This enraged Haman so, that he plotted to kill all Jews in the empire. Queen Esther, a cousin to Mordecai, pleaded with the king to save her people and in the end, Haman was hanged instead of Mordecai.

the VIPs in our yard, trying to kill a chicken by chopping its head off with a dull ax, it really upset me. The chicken managed to run away; it ran all over the yard. The old man was chasing the chicken, and none of the kids helped him. On the contrary, we rooted for the chicken. It took him a while before he managed to catch her and finally chop her head off.

The Kagans were very good customers. Most of the time, they gave us a number of breads or other food in exchange for the meat. We would cut the breads into half-kilo pieces and sell them at the bazaar. Lisa Kagan bought a number of items from us. Once, Mother sold her a beautiful nightgown for a number of breads. Lisa walked with the nightgown in the streets in the middle of the day. She never saw or had anything like it and didn't know what to do with it. These fancy people from the large cities in Russia never saw things that we, from small towns in Poland, had.

Nine

Turkestan was quite a large community. We had a marketplace there, a bazaar, surrounded by a huge wall, where the locals came to sell and buy goods. Of course, everyone else who came to the bazaar also wanted to sell anything they had or buy what they needed. And many just came to see all the different foods they could not afford to buy. For me, watching the people go to the bazaar was intriguing. The streets were full of sand, and you could see the small donkeys loaded up with merchandise. On top of all the merchandise, you would see the Babai sitting while the wife was pulling the donkey, with a small stick poking at the donkey while shouting "Ch, Ch, Ch . . ." to make it move faster in the sand. And so they went until they reached the bazaar. Sometimes, you would see that the load was so high and heavy that the poor little donkey couldn't move; it would fall over with everything on it. And when that happened, they would simply load everything back on the donkey again, the Babai would get back on top, and the process would continue this way until they reached the marketplace. Once they reached the bazaar, the Babai would help unload the donkey and then he would go to the *chai chana*, the teahouse, while the wife remained at the market to sell the merchandise until the end of the day. At the end of the day, the Babai returned to help load what didn't sell, climbed back on the donkey, and the wife would take him home.

In the teahouse, there were professional storytellers who would tell stories of "A Thousand and One Nights" to the men while they sat on small rugs around low tables drinking tea and smoking water pipes.

The marketplace was very interesting. Again, it took you back to the biblical days. For example, they did not sell milk out of jugs. Instead, you would see a small goat or lamb standing. It wasn't really an animal; it was an animal skin cleverly and beautifully sewn together to look as if it were the real animal. The milk was kept in this "animal," and near its nose there was a latch of some sort that they opened and closed to pour the measures of milk to be sold. The women carried everything that needed to be carried on their heads. It was very colorful and fascinating to watch. There were foods there that we had never seen before. They had cantaloupes, which they called *dinye*, the size of watermelons. These *dinye* were cut into long strips, then dried in the sun for days and later braided and sold by the kilo. These sundried melon pieces were used instead of sugar. There were magnificent grapes, some the size of half a finger. But I never saw bananas there. They did have very large watermelons. To show how good they were, the vendor would cut a small triangle deep into the watermelon and pull it out to show how red and ripe it was and the thickness of the rind. The thicker the rind was, the cheaper the watermelon.

The vendors handled thieves on their own. The police were seldom called in. When someone was caught stealing, the crowd began shouting *"Karag! Karag!"* ("Thief! Thief!"). Then, each carrying a stick, the vendors would surround the thief and beat him until he was unable to move. That was the punishment for stealing at the market. There was one man who was called "the *chapper*" (the grabber), who went around grabbing things at the market. He wouldn't even run away. He'd grab a piece of bread and shove it into his mouth, and he didn't care what was done to him. One time, he grabbed a piece of bread from someone in my family and devoured it on the ground. Some of the vendors saw what he did and beat him horribly. Once, I witnessed a beating of "the grabber" that I will never forget. He was beaten so badly that his ears began to detach. The amazing part was that the man did not cry; he did not move. He just lay in the sand with the piece of bread in his mouth.

I was very familiar with the ways of the bazaar because I, myself, went there to sell things a number of times, and I also carefully observed what was going on there. That was when we had sold some beautiful garments to Lisa Kagan in exchange for a number of breads. Whenever we had bread to sell, I would go out to the bazaar to sell it. Of course, my mother, sister, and aunt also sold things there when we needed to, but I really knew what to watch out for. First of all, you had to watch out for the police, because if you were caught, your bread would be confiscated and sometimes they would also arrest you. Secondly, you had to watch out for "the *chapper*." And thirdly, when someone bought something from you, you had to be very careful about how they counted out the money. Very often they would fold the money in half and double-count the bills in their own hand. That way, when they handed you the money, you thought you were getting full payment but were only getting half. I believe my sister was conned that way once. So whenever I sold something, I asked them to count out the money directly into my hand and not in their own. At times you would find people who refused to pay by counting the money into your hand. In fact, one time a Jewish man came over to buy bread from me. When I told him to count out the payment into my hand, he refused; he looked at my bare feet and said to me in Yiddish, "Go crap on your feet and you'll have brown shoes for the holiday." I got angry at him and responded, "Go shit on your own feet and then YOU will have brown shoes for the holiday."

The bazaar was an amazing place to see. It had numerous gated entryways, and near those gates there were always a number of blind Uzbeks sitting and begging. When a passerby gave them something, the Uzbek would bless him, but if a passerby did not give anything, the Uzbek would curse him bitterly. They were even able to follow people around. I had the impression that they were undercover informants; I had seen them take money for information.

Not far from these blind Uzbeks were people selling sunflower seeds out of huge sacks. The vendors used three types of measures for selling these seeds—a small glass, an average glass, and a large glass. I liked watching the way the people ate them. First they put all the seeds in their pocket. Then they would take a handful of seeds and put them in their mouths; crack them, one at a time; eat the seed; and spit out the shell, never touching the seed once it was in the mouth. After a while, of course, we all learned the trick. The only problem was, we couldn't afford to buy the seeds—at least, not often. Being able to buy sunflower seeds was a very special treat. We used to envy the person who could afford to buy these sunflower seeds.

Many times, at the end of the day, my sister and I would go off to the marketplace to look for pits from *uruk* (apricots). The fancy people would spit out the pits, and we would comb the marketplace searching for them. Sometimes, we'd spend hours looking for the pits. Then when we brought them home, we would sit down, take two stones, crack them open, remove the seeds, dry them, and save them. We were already thinking about when the war would end and we'd escape back to Poland. We wanted to keep these pitted seeds as a treat on the train, so we used to put them away and save them.

While we were living in that fancy yard, we slept outside during the summer because the heat indoors was unbearable. Many times it would rain in the middle of the night, and we would grab all the bedding and run inside for the few minutes the rain lasted and then back out again when it stopped. It wasn't too bad, and we got used to it. At about eleven o'clock every night we could hear what sounded like singing. We later learned that this "singing" came from the marketplace. Every night at the bazaar, the religious leader announced in a songlike fashion any item that was lost or forgotten during the day, and the next day the owners would come to get their things, and at times it included an animal. It was very interesting.

In the house, we had a stove that my grandpa built, but it was not used during the summer. We had another stove near the house for the summer. But it was not easy to find things to use as firewood. Wood was a great luxury. There were hardly any trees. So we quickly learned what to do from the locals. We went around and picked up camel droppings. These droppings were used for firewood. For the outside stove it wasn't too bad, but using it inside the house was very unpleasant. Once in a while, on the outskirts of town, because it was desert country, you could find dried cacti flying around. We collected that too to be used as firewood. So when we saw dried cacti, or dried droppings from camels and sometimes from donkeys as well, we would bring them home and put them into the dilapidated barn. We piled up as much as we could. We used the ashes from the stove and mixed them with water to make ink, which we used in school. You had to be creative to make life a little bit easier, or at least bearable.

Hunger was all around us. Our fortunes kept on changing by the week, and often by the day. I was still always hungry, as was everyone else. Grandpa used to say that he wished he could live to see the day that there would be enough food on the table for me to eat. We could see people on the streets on their bellies, crawling to the *pamonei yama*—garbage dump. They had difficulty crawling. They would just stare at you and never say anything. You would see the same people for a number of days. They seldom made it; almost all of them died on the way. People were dying of hunger all over the place. I remember a doctor with his son from Warsaw coming to us many times hoping to get something to eat. Many times my mother added more and more water to the soup so that she would have something to give them. They did not make it. They were too gentle. They could not do physical work, and they perished from hunger. Many times my friends and I would climb up on the few trees on our street and sit on them for hours, licking the leaves that had a sugar coating. And when we saw any kind of grass, anything that looked edible, we would eat it. In some areas in town we had a few acacia trees. When they blossomed, we would pick the flowers and eat them. It was a miracle that we were not poisoned.

Ten

My sister and I went to school every day. We went to Zalesnaya Daroga School (Railroad School). It was not far from our house, and each morning all the classes met on a field in designated areas in front of the school. We had thirty minutes of exercise, and then we marched to our classrooms. My classroom had a portrait hanging of the great Russian hero Bogdan Chmelnitzki, a Cossack who united with the Tartars against Poland. While fighting Poland he committed terrible atrocities against the Jews. Between the years 1648 and 1655 he was responsible for the brutal slaughtering of more than one hundred thousand Jews and leaving almost all the rest of the Jews impoverished.

After about one year, my sister left our school and went to a school called TGZD. Our school periodically checked the students' hair for lice. My sister had very long beautiful hair, and one time they found lice in her hair. After that they kept checking her hair every week and made it an annoying and humiliating experience. With parental permission she was able to change schools. TGZD was a very good school, but very far from our house, and she had to pass a cemetery to get there. Often, very hungry jackals and dogs would dig up graves and scatter the bones. It was very unpleasant to walk there, so my father walked her to school almost every day before going to work.

At my school I was taught reading, writing, arithmetic, geography, patriotism, and love of communism. The teacher devoted the last thirty minutes of every school day to reading stories of patriotism to us. One story that stands out in my mind dealt with a very young *komsomol*, a member of the Young Communist League. This young *komsomol* was playing near a railway line when he suddenly noticed that the rail line was damaged or sabotaged. He had no time to alert the authorities because he could hear a train coming. To save the train, the young *komsomol* cut his hand, smeared his blood on his small handkerchief, and with the bloodied handkerchief flagged down the train to a halt and saved the day. This story made a great impression on all the children, and we all wanted to be heroes.

We were also taught that Lenin and Stalin symbolized Truth and Verity. When swearing to tell the truth they said, "*Chasnaya Lenenskaya*" or "*Chasnaya Stalinskaya*," meaning "Just as Lenin (or Stalin) is true, I am telling the truth." Instead of swearing by G-d, they swore by Stalin or Lenin.

The Railroad School was a good school, not because of the caliber of the students, but because they treated us better. Perhaps that was because many of the students were from families working on the railroad or in government. Every day we would get a tiny piece of bread in the middle of the day. It was the size of a brownie, but we were very happy with it. Sometimes, if a child was out of the classroom when the teacher gave out the bread, the child would lose out because the teacher would take it for herself. She'd be in seventh heaven with the bigger portion of bread to take home. The piece of bread was worth more to her than anything else.

When my sister and I would leave for school in the mornings we would take something with us, most of the time a piece of bread. Then, along the way, some big boys would stop us and search our little schoolbags. They never searched for money or possessions; they searched for one thing only—food. When they found either a piece of bread or a fruit or two in our bag, they took some of it— never all of it. If you had a piece of bread, they broke it and took half; if you had two fruits, they took one. Though their hunger was great, they did not take all of your food away. You couldn't help but feel for them; everybody was just trying to survive.

While everyone was suffering from hunger, the high officials in our courtyard lived in luxury. There were two families, the Yogodas and the Kagans, whose sons I was friendly with. Mr. Yogoda, the head of the NKVD, as you remember, had two sons, and I was friends with Fema, the older one. He did not have too many friends to play with and usually stayed home with his brother. His parents permitted him to play with me many times but seldom invited me into their house. I liked being in their home because whenever Fema's mother would give him and his brother something to eat, she would give me something too. I remember sacks of walnuts, which were a real luxury, lying under their beds. They had all kinds of things. Fema and I went to the same school. Many times he could not eat the sandwich he brought from home but was afraid to take it back—so he used to give it to me. I used to meet him at the second floor stairwell door, where he would sneak the sandwich to me so that no one would see, and I would very quickly take it from him and disappear. He was happy to get rid of it, and I was even happier to get it.

I was also friendly with the Kagan family. As the war went on, practically everyone was drafted into the army. The Kagans had a son also named Fema. He was very tall, over six feet, whereas I was a young boy of ten or eleven at that time, and short. Fema was kept locked in the house because his parents paid a fortune to keep him out of the army. He was their only child, and his family was afraid he'd be seen and reported. But once in a while he wanted to get out of his cage, and the place he wanted to go many times was to a movie. His parents were afraid to send him alone, so his mother would ask me to go with him. I, of course, gladly went because I got a free ticket plus a treat—a candy or a *pranick*, a sugar-coated cookie. I used to look forward to this. I had it a little bit better than my sister. I would sometimes get something extra; she never got anything.

Food was always on my mind. I think that there is nothing worse than hunger—not even death. When you are dead, you feel nothing and are relieved of all suffering. When you are alive you need food. If I did not have family chores after school and on school holidays I used to hang out with my friends who had as much or even less than I did. We always thought about how to get something to eat. My friend Toly, who was older, was the group leader. We each had a slingshot, which we made ourselves and used to kill birds. Then we would make a fire so that we could grill them and eat what we could. One day we found a porcupine. We were sure we would have a good meal that day. After we killed it we put it on the fire to grill. Once its hair burned off there was virtually nothing left. We were very disappointed.

Many times we would go to the station to see if we would be lucky that day. When luck was with us, trains with open cars went by carrying "oil cake"—a cake or mass of cottonseeds from which the oil has been pressed. Normally, it is fed to cattle and sheep and is also used as soil fertilizer. But we would steal some of these "cakes" and bring them home to eat. These oil cakes were big, rectangular, yellowish chips that were about two inches thick. We had no problem eating this; we even enjoyed them.

The more daring ones in our group would take a wire about three feet long, bend the tip about two inches, and walk in the street and look for women going to the bazaar carrying fruit on their heads. Then, if no one was watching, they would pick off some fruit with the wire and disappear. It was very dangerous; anyone caught doing that would get an extremely severe beating.

In Russia, you had to learn how to play the game. Even if you had money or enough bread and butter, you could not permit anyone to know. You had to be careful of your own children, for if they said anything at school about money or the black market the police would be informed immediately.

After about a year the authorities removed a few families who lived in our backyard. Their apartments were turned into a *stolova*—a restaurant and a small store that distributed bread. The store made it much easier for us to stay on the bread lines because it enabled us to switch off with each other on the long lines. Those with special cards were able to get some food in the restaurant. The special cards were given to pensioners and to parents or wives of sons and husbands in the army. The meal in the restaurant was soup with a small piece of turtle meat most of the time. Truckloads of live turtles were brought in, and the restaurant workers used to sit and pull out each turtle's head with a fork, then cut it off and throw it away. Those with the special cards stood on line for as long as three hours to get their soup and turtle meat.

Mr. Koslov, who lived in our courtyard, had a card for the restaurant. He stood on line for hours to get the soup, which was more water than soup. He brought it home and then quietly brought it to us for my dog, Bobik. Many times I shared it with Bobik or someone else in the family. Mr. Koslov had a lot of gold coins, and often he approached members of my family to see if we could sell some of them for him. He bought all of his food on the black market, yet he stood on line for two or three hours every day to get that soup. He had to go along and play the game.

Some of the locals were not better off than we were. There was a girl, Camilla, the daughter of one of our neighbors, who would go up on her rooftop when she was hungry, and she would often sing and dance and play the cymbals to forget her hunger. She would dance for about an hour at a time, then come back down. But she would still be hungry. I can still remember the melody of her song. It was always the same song and dance.

Camilla lived in the same courtyard as my deceased Aunt Feiga's brother, Mottel, and two sisters, Breindel and Reizel. None of them were married, and the three of them lived together in a small *kibidka* on a poor Uzbek's property. Mottel was an expert engraver, a true artist in his field. He was the only one who was able to engrave tombstones. The two sisters were dressmakers. One particular incident involving Mottel stands out in my mind. There was a very large deep hole in a corner of their yard that was kept covered and used as an outhouse. One evening Mottel was walking in the yard and fell into the hole. He began drowning in the dung and started screaming for help. Finally he was heard and was pulled out. My uncle and his sisters worked very hard to clean him up.

Breindel and Reizel were very nice and came to our house many times. Reizel was friendly and outgoing, whereas Breindel was quiet and a loner. She generally liked staying home. Reizel was the prettier sister and let it be known that she wanted to get married. Breindel never spoke of marriage and without anyone knowing, she was quietly having a romance with a traditional young man who lived nearby. He would only come to their house when Breindel was alone. Even Mottel and Reizel didn't know about this romance. When they did learn of it, it was too late. Breindel was already pregnant. The young man was urged, implored, and even threatened to marry her, but he refused. Her entire family was embarrassed and devastated. To them it was a major tragedy, and Mottel and Reizel tried to suppress this news. They managed to arrange for Breindel to stay in a *kolkhoz* for as long as necessary. Months later Breindel returned home all alone.

Eleven

In my house, religion was always part of our lives. My grandpa was orthodox, with a long beard and the traditional side curls. He prayed three times a day. My grandma always had her hair covered. Nonkosher meat never entered our home, even during the terrible times. Grandpa helped establish and maintain the little synagogue regardless of the danger. The synagogue functioned well. Only once, a Russian who claimed to have been drunk got in there. He began shouting anti-Semitic slogans and using profane language. He also managed to rip a piece of the Torah scroll. He was immediately arrested and eventually sentenced to at least one year in prison.

Anti-Semitism was against the law in Russia. If someone made an anti-Semitic remark openly, he would be punished by the authorities. Officially, anti-Semitism was prohibited. Unofficially, there was plenty of it, just as in many other countries.

My father and uncle prayed at home. They feared going to the synagogue, and they did not have the time it would have taken. Throughout the war I was given religious instruction as often as possible. In Siberia, after recuperating, I received instructions in reading Hebrew from a prayer book once or twice a week. My teacher was an elderly man who was a *melamed*, a religious teacher by profession. He was paid with food. Even though we had so little, mother insisted that she would do with less, but I must get a religious education. "He is not a *goy*," (a person of another nation or non-religious Jew) my mother would say, and my father concurred. I continued receiving instruction in prayer book and Bible in Turkestan for about two years, and then I was sent to a more advanced teacher to learn Torah with Rashi commentary. All this was done in secret. This teacher did not come to my house. I had to go to him, and no one was to know about it. My Bible I would carry under my shirt so that no one, not even my friends, would know about it. Religious instruction was prohibited.

While we were in Turkestan we baked matzoth every year for Passover. Grandpa and other elderly Jews, with the mediation of a Bukhara Jew, rented a place that had a water well in the yard, an oven on the ground floor, and, several steps up, a large room where mostly women, including Grandma, kneaded dough and rolled the matzoth. Men only would bake them. The process from the start of kneading the dough until the matzoth were finished baking took not more than eighteen minutes. Everything was carefully and strictly observed. I remember the *lott*, the place where the matzoth were baked. I was there many times with Grandpa, helping him out. Very few things could keep Grandpa from observing the religious laws, customs, and ceremonies. He was a fearless man, but we always worried that he might endanger his life and ours.

To see Grandpa in a *tallith* and *tefillin*, the prayer shawl and phylacteries, at the window or open door was nothing out of ordinary for any of us. But the first time the chief of the NKVD saw him he almost fell back. He knew what it was, but he probably hadn't seen anyone with a *tallith* and *tefillin* in G-d knows how many years. His wife told mother that she was the granddaughter of a *shochet*.

Mr. Yogoda used to call Grandpa "Komsomol," which meant a member in the Young Communist League. These were people who would inform on their own parents if they had done something against Communist teachings. He was fond of Grandpa and used to speak to him whenever the opportunity arose. Maybe Grandpa reminded him of his own grandfather. For a chief of the NKVD, a true Communist, to show friendship to an orthodox Jew was extraordinary. After all, as Vladimir Lennon said, "Religion is the opiate of the masses."

It must have been at the end of 1943 when one evening we saw Mr. Yogoda walking around in the yard, close to our house. We saw him trying to get the attention of someone in our house, so Grandpa walked outside. At that point Mr. Yogoda called out to him, "*Komsomol chady suda*," meaning, "Come over here." Grandpa walked over, and they began walking to the side of the house, talking. Mr. Yogoda asked Grandpa to make arrangements to have his two boys circumcised—not immediately, but in the near future. At that time his older son was about ten years old and his younger one about seven. This decision entailed a great deal of danger for the top man of the NKVD and some danger for Grandpa. Grandpa was very surprised at this request. He asked no questions, but he was very pleased and promised that he would be very careful not to tell anyone. He would try to make all the necessary arrangements and would keep Mr. Yogoda informed. This was no easy task.

Grandpa had to find a man who was both a proper *mohel* (one who performs ritual circumcisions) and a responsible person, while Mr. Yogoda had to find the appropriate time. Grandpa kept his promise. He found the right *mohel* and informed Mr. Yogoda at the beginning of 1944, but Mr. Yogoda hesitated. He did not think that the time was appropriate. In February or March Grandpa became very ill, and the plans for the circumcisions were postponed. Grandpa was an extremely strong man. In all his life, he was never sick. If he had a toothache, it was a tragedy for him, and suddenly he became very sick and could not accept it. I remember it very vividly. It was Passover of 1944. We were preparing for the Seder, and Grandpa ignored his illness and his fever. He went down barefoot on the floor, washed himself, and sat at the Seder as if nothing was wrong. But unfortunately, a lot of things were wrong. He was getting worse. The doctor was called, but there were no medicines to be had. He made it through seven days of Passover, and on the last day we called the doctor again. I still remember the doctor. He was short, heavyset, and had a limp. We always called him the *krumer doktor*—"the doctor with the limp." He never suggested putting Grandpa into the hospital because the hospital couldn't help anyone; it had no medicines, and very few people who went into the hospital came out alive. The doctor gave Grandpa some kind of injection and said, "He's better off this way. He will not suffer so much." Grandpa Yitzhak died on April 24, 1944, the last day of Passover.

The preparations for burial, which is to purify the body by following ritual cleansing procedures and to dress it in shrouds, took place in our own house. I'll never forget that. He was buried in the cemetery next to my aunt and my cousin. I am sure the cemetery is there today and that Grandpa's gravestone and the gravestones of my aunt and cousin are standing as well. When my uncle built their gravestones, they were like fortresses.

Grandpa was in his late sixties when he died. Yogoda's sons never got circumcised. My Grandpa's dream of seeing me sit at the table and watching me eat as much as I wanted was something he did not live to see. It was a very bad year. A few months after we lost Grandpa, my sister Beatrice became very ill. She contracted typhus. I remember that Mother had to cut her hair. Beatrice had very long, beautiful, blond hair. We kept her braid of hair for many years. She did not go to the hospital. We cared for her at home. Beatrice was very fortunate that she came out of this alive and well. The great majority of people who contracted this dreadful disease, which is transmitted by lice and fleas, never made it. Typhus was one of the biggest killers.

As the war continued, and Hitler made progress coming deeper and deeper into Russia, a number of things happened where we were. The locals began showing their true colors. They began attacking Jews in the streets. If you showed any sign of weakness or ran away, that would be the end of you. But if you stood up to them and fought back, they left you alone.

The other thing was the preparation for a planned pogrom on the Jews in our city. One morning when we woke up the town was without police, without government workers, and without railway workers. We did not know what happened. Only a few days later we discovered the reason. It seemed that a group of anti-Semites made preparations for a pogrom. The preparations reached the stage where streets were divided up among different workers. They knew the houses where the Jews lived and even the time when the slaughter would take place. Somehow this plan was brought before a very high official in Chimkent. When he saw the plan he showed great interest and wanted to implement the same type of plan in his town. He asked for twenty-four or forty-eight hours to think about it. That night he put in a telephone call to the top Russian leaders. That same night Stalin sent in his people, and our city was emptied of all those that I mentioned previously. It took about a week before they were all replaced. Thanks to the individual from Chimkent, who, according to the story, was of Jewish descent, thousands of lives were saved.

What Mr. Yogoda did at this time, we do not know. It is possible that the NKVD that was involved in the planning of the pogrom was only in our town, in the lower echelon. And he, perhaps, with the people Stalin sent down, participated in cleaning out, arresting, and deporting all those involved to Siberia. Mr. Yogoda remained in his post until the end of the war, when he returned to Leningrad with his family.

Twelve

Life in Turkistan was never dull. Something was always happening—sometimes even funny things. The huge bazaar was the nerve center of the town. It was one of the main attractions. You always expected something to happen, and you were seldom disappointed.

One day while Grandma was at the bazaar the authorities encircled the market and began to inspect documents. Since Grandma had neither Russian documents nor Russian citizenship papers, she got arrested. She was taken to the police station and not permitted out until the whole family accepted Russian citizenship. With no other choice, we became temporary citizens of the USSR. Every six months we renewed our citizenship.

At another time, during cotton picking season, there was a shortage of laborers. The authorities encircled the bazaar and took truckloads of people away to the cotton fields to pick cotton for the day. Meanwhile, the families of these people were not made aware of what happened to them and were worried sick until the end of the day, when everyone was brought back to town. The Russians considered these events as small *oblavas*, which were raids or kidnappings.

On a lighter side, one day while I was at the bazaar, a Russian truck driver, driving an American truck, a Studebaker, drove into the middle of the marketplace. He shut off the engine, came out, stood on top of the hood, and showed everybody a little key. "*Smotry* . . . ," he said. "Look, look at this key. This little key can turn on this mighty American truck!" By this time hundreds of people, adults and children, had gathered around the truck. He then got into the truck, put the key into the ignition, and started the engine. It was an amazing thing to see. There was no need to turn the crankshaft for ten minutes before starting the engine. Everybody was clapping as he began moving with the truck and kicking up a huge dust cloud. People were running after him in the dust commenting, "Only the Americantze can do things like that."

As the war intensified, the Russians began carrying out real *oblavas*, literally raiding homes and kidnapping able-bodied men to the *trudovoy front*—work behind the front lines. Very seldom did anyone return alive from there. These raids were mostly carried out in the middle of the night. Only sometimes they would sweep through the neighborhood during the day, looking for people who did not work. My uncle, because he was an excellent builder, was able to obtain letters stating how important he was to his place of work. For my father, it was impossible. He was a laborer. But we also knew of cases where the letters did not help, so my father and uncle began taking all kinds of precautionary measures not to be caught.

The small room in our house had a wooden floor. My uncle cut out a square in that floor. We dug a hole for one person to fit into, standing upright, in the event of an emergency. The dirt was carried out at night, some into the garden, which we had right near the house, but most of it was carried into the dilapidated barn. This way no one would see that we were digging anything. The square was cut out so perfectly that it wasn't visible.

Mr. Yagoda proved himself to be a good friend. He saved Father and Uncle a number of times. He knew when the *oblava* would take place, and he would use a code to let us know. He'd pass by our house and say to any of the adults in my family, "It will be joyful tonight." This was code for "They are coming tonight." With this information, they knew that they should not spend the night at home. My father and uncle were very well liked by the people they worked for because their work was excellent and they fixed many things at their homes free of charge. The person in charge where they worked was a woman called Shura. When Father knew that there was going to be a raid, he and Uncle would go to Shura, and she would lock them up in the government store for the night. Other times, when Shura was unavailable or unable to help, they would go to another woman called Chochlova, and she too would hide them in a government building for the night. But there were also times when Father and Uncle would not be tipped off and would hear a commotion in the middle of the night—they knew it was an *oblava*. They would quickly get out of the house, crawl on the outside walls to a nearby tall building, get on its roof, and climb through a small window into its attic. It must have been a government building. And from their position, they were able to observe what was going on all around. Sometimes they were able to see the groups going from house to house looking for people. Father and Uncle would wait until dawn and then return home.

One day, my father was home. It was in the middle of the day . . . I don't know why he was home; maybe he was ill. Suddenly, from out of nowhere, we had an *oblava*. Father saw them through the window, but more importantly, someone also noticed him. Without any hesitation, Father went into the secret hiding place under the floor. The authorities came into the house and searched everywhere. They turned the place upside down, and the official kept saying he was positive he saw a man. We told them that everyone was at work; no one was at home. They went through the house knocking on the wooden floor with a stick, but they did not find Father. Finally, the authorities had no choice but to leave. And once again, we couldn't help but wonder about the role the Rebbe's coins played in saving Father . . . the two coins he had given to Father that were meant to protect him and have G-d watch over him.

After Grandpa passed away, Uncle did everything in his power to say Kaddish. It is a prayer for the dead, and for a parent it is recited at every service of every day for eleven months following the parent's death. It is necessary to have a *minyan*, that is, ten Jewish men present, in order to recite this prayer. In our family, not to say Kaddish would have been considered tragic, and Uncle would not have been able to live with himself. The only place to say Kaddish was at the little synagogue, and he tried very hard to say it as often as possible. As I had mentioned earlier, the authorities kept an eye on who was entering to worship. Uncle used to go through strangers' yards, climb walls, and go through back alleys in order to get inside without being noticed. Once, on his way to the synagogue, an *oblava* started, and he was caught just before he entered. He presented his documents and papers showing that he was an important worker, but nothing helped. The people where he worked tried their best, but they also could not help him. Uncle was taken to the city of Turkistan with all the other people caught that day.

We knew very few people there. One person we knew was my mother's distant cousin, Chayke. She was a very beautiful young woman. She was from a very poor family in Krylov. Her parents married her off at a very young age to a man learning to become a barber. His name was Bookie and could not have been more than eighteen years old. He looked like a *nebbish*, a nerd, whereas she looked like an actress. People knew this match would not last. They did have a son together, but she could not live with Bookie and left him. Chayke knew the top people in the government. She obviously had affairs with some of them. She was quite a woman and got around.

Mother and Grandma ran to see her. They told Chayke what happened and that she was their last hope. Chayke was a very kind-hearted person and promised to do her best. She dressed up and went to see the top official. We never knew what transpired between Chayke and the official she met with on my uncle's behalf, but a few hours later my uncle was released. What the officials were not able to do for Uncle, cousin Chayke was able to accomplish. We were very thankful to her. There was no end to our joy at my uncle's release. And despite this scare, Uncle continued trying to go say Kaddish as much as possible.

At some point in 1944 the *oblavas* stopped, and we were both relieved and grateful. But life did not improve much. It was a little better for us because of our connections, but we were still hungry. I neither stopped collecting the pits with my sister at the bazaar nor did I stop stealing oil cakes from the trains at the station. I was still dreaming of food. Once, my dream was fulfilled; it was when my aunt was assigned to a small store to cut and distribute watermelon. Being that she was alone in the store, I was able to get in and sit under the table where no one else would see me. I ate as much watermelon as I wanted. In fact, I ate so much that I was unable to move. By the end of the day I walked around with a big belly and very happy. This satisfaction was like a dream. It was great at the time, but by the next day I was hungry again.

After all this time in Turkistan, we still had great difficulty coping with the heat. In the middle of the day the temperature rose well above 100°F. We walked around barefoot, and the soles of my feet were so thick that I could walk on glass and not feel it. Yet in the middle of the day it was impossible to walk because the sand got particularly hot, and the sand was everywhere. If one had to go out in the middle of the day, he would carry a pitcher of water to spill on the sand before stepping down. Even the local children had to walk that way. But there was no humidity there. Before my father would come home from work, we would take a pail, fill it up with water, and put it in the sun. When he got home he had warm water for washing up. If we had watermelon, we would lower some of it into the water well and keep it there for a couple of hours, and we would have cool watermelon for my father and uncle. The locals were amazing in the heat. They walked around fully dressed and with fur coats on. They claimed it kept the heat away from them. Additionally, they wore leather boots, and if that was not enough, they sat and drank hot tea. We, on the other hand, could not stand to have anything on because we were so hot. There was no breeze; the air did not move. It was very still; not a single leaf moved. Yet, all of a sudden, from out of nowhere, a sandstorm would hit. The sandstorms were so strong that small stones would fly through the air. I had a problem breathing, so I learned that when a sandstorm hit while I was outside, I had to throw myself on the ground face down and wait for it to blow over. The sandstorms occurred once or twice a week, only during the summer. In the wintertime we would get snow once in a while. We loved it, but the locals hated it. They used to blame us for the snow and cold weather, saying that we brought it to the area.

Life in Turkistan was anything but easy. For example, most of the year we walked around barefoot, and it was difficult. The shoes we had, we tried to save for the winter. Of course nothing was thrown out. I always had a great desire for boots; I always envied people who had them. I remember that once, my parents bought me a pair of boots. In the winter, I put on the boots and I went outside. Not far from our house was a little hill, and all the kids would go there to "ski" or "skate." But there were no skis or skates, so how did we do it? Well, in order to ski, we would take a piece of wood, clear it well, and stand on it going downhill. The hill was small. To skate we would just use our shoes for sliding down that hill. I was sliding down on my new boots, and before I knew it, after going down two or three times, I noticed the soles were gone. It was all fake. When the boots were made, they looked very good on the outside, but the sole consisted of a piece of cardboard covered with a very thin layer of leather. It was a great disappointment and very expensive for my parents. The man who made these lived on the other side of the wall from us.

A number of months later I had the opportunity to get back at him, but of course, I was not permitted. What happened was that we were out in the backyard playing, and suddenly, we saw things come flying over the wall. We saw all kinds of boots, leather, nails, and an assortment of other things. We didn't know from where it was coming. We collected everything, looked at it, but didn't know what to do. A number of hours later, we found out what took place. It seemed that somebody informed on this shoemaker that he was making boots and shoes and selling them on the black market. When he was tipped off that his house was going to be raided, he began throwing everything he had in his house over the wall. We collected everything, but at the insistence of our parents, we returned it all. I, of course, was not happy with this, as I still remembered my boots.

Thirteen

In about the middle of 1944, the Polish Jews in town got bolder. For Rosh Hashana and Yom Kippur the little synagogue was not sufficient. A Babai rented them a house with a yard to conduct services. Most, if not all, Polish Jews attended. The services were led by Haskale, a rabbinical student from Poland. Some people said he was a rabbi. He had a very nice voice. This Haskale made a very nice living by dealing on the black market. He was in the big league. He dealt with gold coins and precious gems. Father introduced Mr. Kozlow to him, and he bought gold coins from Mr. Kozlow a number of times. There was a rumor that Haskale was taken for a ride by someone. According to the story, a man approached him with a little pouch full of gold coins at the bazaar. They walked around talking about the merchandise. The man took out one gold coin and gave it to him to inspect. After Haskale inspected the coin, they made a deal. Haskale took the little pouch, looked in very quickly, and put the pouch into his pocket so no one would see. When he came home, he opened the pouch and discovered to his chagrin that only the coin that he was shown was real gold. All the others were fakes. There was not much he could do about it. Black marketeering was a high crime; he could not go to the police. He had to keep his mouth shut. The only thing he could do was to be more careful next time. As a cantor, he was good. Everyone loved his chanting of the prayers.

Russian Jews seldom came to pray. The great majority were not religious, and the rest feared the authorities. I remember Mrs. Yagoda being in our home once. She saw a *siddur* (prayer book) on the table. She opened the *siddur* and showed mother how beautifully she was able to read. She had no desire to go to services, even on Yom Kippur, but she and the others fasted on Yom Kippur.

It was on a snowy February day of 1945 that mother went to the hospital and gave birth to a baby girl. We were all a little disappointed. We hoped for a boy so we could name him for Grandpa Yitzhak. But it was not to be. We Ashkenazim (northern and central European Jews) name after deceased; Sephardim (southwestern European and Middle Eastern Jews) name for living people. In ancient Israel as well as modern day Israel, Jews name after events as well as people. The baby girl was named Chaya, Chayke in Yiddish, after my great-great-grandmother who lived to be 106. We loved the baby very much. To raise a child in those days was very, very difficult. There was very little that one could provide for the baby, but everybody chipped in, and we tried to do the best that we could for the infant under the circumstances.

I can still recall how we tried to make diapers for her. There were no such things as diapers in those days in Turkistan. We could not get the material to make them. So what we did was to use Father's *onetezes*—these were like small scarves Father used to wrap around his feet instead of socks—and anything we had or could spare would be cut up for diapers for little Chaya. In the beginning, of course, my mother nursed her, and we had to see to it that Mother would be able to eat half-decently so she could nurse the baby. The entire family came through beautifully; everybody did whatever they could. We saw to it that Mother should have a little bit more, and it worked beautifully, and little Chaya progressed very nicely.

Fourteen

All during the war we neither heard nor knew of what was happening in Poland and in the other occupied lands. The news we
heard on the loudspeakers from a radio coming from the post
office never spoke of Nazi atrocities. Polish Jews were encouraged
to go one or two evenings a week to the Communist clubs to hear
a government official explain the economic system, the newspaper
articles, and the news of the day. Father, Uncle, and many other
people went to these clubs to show that they were willing to learn.
They never mentioned Auschwitz, Majdanek, Treblinka, or the
Warsaw Ghetto Uprising. We never heard that the Germans were
slaughtering Russian soldiers in the hundreds of thousands if not
in the millions. We were never told about Babi Yar. We had newspapers in these clubs and in other places—the *Pravda*, which
means the truth, and the *Izvestya*, which means the news—but the
problem was that the *Pravda* never printed the truth, and the
Izvestya never printed the news. It was against government policy.
We were always kept in the dark. We seldom heard mentioned
that the Russians were losing, only that they were retreating to
strategic points.

Every day we heard that the Russian forces were taking forty or fifty *naselone punkte* (strategic points). The only time we heard the truth was when Stalin came on the radio with a crying voice saying, "*Moskva vaposnosty*" ("Moscow is in danger."), and he asked the Russian people to fight for Mother Russia, not for communism. It was a very sad day. He himself was already in Kuybyshev.

The war was winding down. No more German soldiers on Russian soil. It must have been in March of 1945 that a local soldier returned with one leg amputated. He was standing in front of the movie house talking to a crowd of people. He was telling about the horrors of the war and what Hitler was doing to the Jews. Nobody wanted to believe. He told about death marches—we heard and we couldn't believe. Father was totally confused. He did not want to believe what he heard. He remembered the Germans in World War I; he remembered some people were killed when they came in, but they were not murderers. This is what he hoped in his heart.

In the meantime, in our backyard, the chief of the NKVD and his family and his brother-in-law and his family moved back home to Leningrad. A few other families in our yard went back to Charkov and other cities. After they left, the authorities began making changes in our backyard. They built a wall right in the middle, separating our little house from the main buildings. We could no longer use the Pyervamiskaya address; it had become a side street. The area where the big shots lived was changed around. They added all kinds of things. They added on to the restaurant; they added stores, etc. Things were not the same anymore. We hoped that soon maybe we, too, would be able to go home to our family.

May 7, 1945, was the unconditional surrender of Germany to the Allied forces. Everybody was very happy. We hoped that our suffering would soon be over and we'd be reunited with our family in Poland. We wanted to tell them all about our struggle for survival and of those in our family who did not survive. We began going to the station in the late afternoon hoping to meet someone or see someone who would be able to tell us some news from home.

In June and July, thousands of Russian troops began passing through Turkestan toward the Chinese border. Some of the men were lightly wounded, and some were on crutches. We could not understand what was going on. At the same time we saw many transports passing from occupied areas, carrying everything from doorknobs to machinery.

On one occasion, somebody came running to our house telling us that there was an Isaac Bichler at the station waiting. We thought, wow, maybe it's my father's brother, so we ran with great hope in our hearts. It was a distant cousin of my father's who had the same name as my uncle, Isaac Bichler, and he told us that he had not been on the front and he too did not know much about what was going on because he and his family were living in Uzbekistan. He had not seen anyone, and the Russians were sending him to Manchuria.

Many people made a nice few rubles during this time. Some of the soldiers passing through, depending on where they were coming from, had lots of things to sell, especially watches. These watches were taken from captured and dead German soldiers. Some of these Russian soldiers had both of their arms covered with watches that they tried to sell, mostly for vodka. There were some people who took bottles of vodka that they diluted with water and sold to the soldiers. Sometimes, they even sealed bottles of water and sold them to the soldiers as vodka for watches. People conducted business in all kinds of ways, and it became a regular pastime for us to go down to the station to watch the goings-on while hoping and praying that we would meet someone who could tell us about our family.

Father and Uncle kept on going to the station after work or on Sundays to observe the behavior of the Russian authorities. They wanted to see whether the Russians were guarding the area rigidly or whether it was possible to get on the trains. They just wanted to see what was going on. And this they kept on doing for a number of months. They first began their surveillance right after the war was over; they kept a close watch of what was happening at the station and were constantly trying to figure out how it would be possible to arrange an escape. It must have been June or July that my uncle and my father came to the conclusion that we had to try and sell off everything, accumulate a certain amount of money, and then try to escape. We knew this would be very difficult, but we had to try to get out. Every day, it got worse and worse for my father. The war was over, and he still did not hear anything from anyone in his family; this man was torn. It was pulling him to go back home; he just could not take it any longer. He became very nervous, and all his energy was directed towards one thing: the escape. There wasn't an evening that the escape was not discussed. Many times they would take along the children to the station; this was for precautionary measures. The authorities were less suspicious of people walking around with children than of adults walking around alone observing the goings-on. We needed to know what trains were stopping and how long they stood at the station. Were the Russian police watching? Were there secret agents? Who was in control? And, was it possible to pay anyone off?

To escape from Russia was easier said than done. We were about four to five thousand miles away from our home in Poland. To get on a train and try to escape was one thing, but to survive the journey on that train was a whole other issue. How would we obtain food for such a long journey? How much food could we take with us? First of all, there was very little food to take. We could take some bread, some dried bread, but how much could you take? How would we survive? How long would the journey be? After all, we were dealing with a family of nine; we had my parents, my two sisters and myself, Grandma Shifra, Uncle Yeshayahu, his daughter Chaya, and Aunt Rivka. To move and feed nine people was a difficult task, so we had to plan every move very meticulously. Those who had bread cards in Russia were eligible to receive a certain ration of bread every week, and these cards were valid in every government store throughout Russia. If we were able to get such bread cards part of our problems would be solved, but how would we get our hands on such cards? These bread ration cards would be good for at least one month. My father and uncle knew certain individuals in influential places, but how would they convince these people to have the cards issued to us? They themselves did not issue them and would have to convince a third party to do it. One person we knew who had the influence to obtain the bread ration cards for us was a Bukhara Jew named Solomon Hajayoff. Mr. Hajayoff was a very high government official who oversaw a large government company where Uncle and Father worked many times. He was a very nice person, and we believed he was a traditional Jew. He lived in the city. Uncle and Father decided to approach him and tell him the truth; they felt that he was trustworthy. But how to approach a person like Mr. Hajayoff? You had to come in with something. We still had one thing that we hadn't sold that was special. My uncle had a bedspread made with gold and silver threads that he had received as a wedding gift. It was very beautiful and extremely expensive. It was decided that they would present him with this gift and then ask for the favor. If this plan worked, we could start thinking of escaping. If it did not, we'd have to come up with something else.

One day, Father and Uncle approached Mr. Hajayoff and asked him if it would be possible to see him at his home. He smiled—I remember father telling us—and he told them more or less when.

Father and Uncle went, and they presented him and his wife with the gift. She was extremely happy with the gift, and then came the big question—what can I do for you?

Father and Uncle decided to tell him the truth and let him in on the secret that we were planning to escape in order to see what happened to our family. They also told him that they trusted him and could tell him because he was a fellow Jew and they were sure that he would help us as much as possible. Finally, they asked if it was possible for him to use his influence to help obtain bread cards for us.

Mr. Hajayoff listened to everything they told him and promised that he would try. He wanted to give back the gift because he was not positive whether he could fulfill this request. My uncle and father refused to take it; they said it was a gift for Mrs. Hajayoff and not a payoff for the bread cards. Uncle and Father left the house, hoping and praying that this man would come through for us. While waiting for an answer, we sold off whatever we could in a manner that would not arouse suspicion from anyone. We also dried whatever bread we could spare for the journey. Within a number of weeks, Mr. Hajayoff got back to us with the good news that he would be able to obtain the bread cards. He did, and we were very thankful. I don't think that a person winning the lottery would be as happy as we were with those cards. We had to move very swiftly. We began spending more time at the station, watching and looking. At the same time, we were selling everything we could to accumulate as much money as possible. We had to make sure that we could move at a moment's notice with almost no baggage. We even took steps to provide for the safety of my little dog, Bobik. My uncle knew a local from work and told him some story, and he took the dog. It made me feel much better to know that the dog was being cared for.

It was Rosh Hashanah, 1945. We went to pray with all the other Polish Jews as we did in 1944. This Rosh Hashanah was different; the war in Europe was over. However, we still knew nothing about our family. On the second day of Rosh Hashanah, someone came and told us that at the station stopped a *shalon*, a transport with seven cars carrying supplies to Russian troops in Germany. These seven cars were attached to many other cars carrying all kinds of cargo, forming this very long *shalon*. Father and Uncle ran to the station to see if it was possible to make a deal.

They met the lieutenant who was in command and asked if he was willing to take nine people to Poland. The lieutenant, after consulting with the other six soldiers he commanded, said it was feasible for a certain price. Very quickly they agreed on a price. Uncle and Father hurried back home. Within minutes, the entire family was ready. We took what we had in our hands, and we walked to the station. We were happy that we were able to leave on Rosh Hashanah, because we knew that there were fewer police and secret agents watching the station. It was a major holiday; we did not think they expected Jews to leave or try to escape on this day. We took advantage of that, and it worked for us. We came to the station without panic, so as not to arouse any suspicion. We quickly got into the cattle car with the soldiers.

There was a lieutenant, Mesha; there was a corporal, Vanya; and five other soldiers. What they did was, they divided the car in two—half was for them, the other half was for us. There were planks in the middle, separating the upper and the lower parts, like the ground floor and the first floor. Part of our family was on the first floor and the other part on the ground floor; we had total control of half of that wagon, and the soldiers had their side of the wagon. Once we got to Poland, and only Poland, they were to drop us off. These were the arrangements.

Perhaps the happiest of all was my father, because finally, he would be able to get back to his family. With this great hope, we began this very long journey home. The second day of Rosh Hashanah—September 9, 1945—I shall never forget as long as I live.

In the middle of the wagon, we had a metal stove, and there was also a hole in the floor for the toilet. We draped some cloth around it so a person could go in and have a little bit of privacy, and that was all that we had in there. There were four windows in this car; two were on our side and two on the soldiers' side. We, the kids, always liked to sit on top and look out of these windows because we could see out, but no one could see in from the outside. It was very difficult for Grandma to go up, so she was on the lower floor, and we hoped that from then on, everything would be fine.

Fifteen

The first few days on the train were very exciting for us. We were all very hyper. There was excitement and joy in our hearts and in the air. We had a feeling of a great accomplishment. We managed to outsmart the authorities, and that was not done very often in the USSR. As the train moved, the soldiers would open the door, sometimes on both sides of the car. It was warm, and many times, they would take their machine guns with the seventy-two bullets and they would just fire at birds or other objects. It was for target practice and out of boredom. I enjoyed watching and being so close to real soldiers. For my father, it brought back memories of his years in the Polish army. He was very proud of his service. We could tell that he would have enjoyed firing off a few shots, but he was embarrassed to ask. There were times the soldiers would climb up on the roof of the car while the train was in motion. Some of them slept there; some played cards. They didn't know what to do with themselves. But after a while, things began looking bleak. At the beginning, we traveled for a few days without stopping, but then, our train started making frequent stops. At times when we got into a station we would remain one or two days, sometimes even three days. This began worrying us because every day we would consume a certain amount of food, but we didn't know how long it would last. If the train stopped at a small station, we didn't dare go outside and risk being seen, and the door was not opened. This was, after all, a military transport, and if the authorities noticed us, the soldiers and we would end up in a slave labor camp in Siberia for the rest of our lives. So all of these things had to be taken into consideration. The soldiers had to be very careful as well. We were convinced that the corporal, Vanya, a nice-looking fellow, was Jewish. He sort of kept a vigilant eye on us. He made sure that the other soldiers behaved properly. He smiled at us, and you could see that he cared. We could feel it in our bones that he felt a certain kinship to us, and he watched over us. We worried, but on the other hand, we were also extremely happy because we felt that an end to our suffering was near. We thought soon, soon, a week, two, three, we'd be home; we'd be with our relatives, and we'd be able to tell them about all the misery, all our sufferings, and all our tragedies. We'd tell them of the hunger, the starvation, and the disease that befell us. Little did we know what was really happening in Poland. But at least it was good that we had this hope. It was this hope of seeing them that kept my father alive and well.

As the journey continued, we had to do certain things to stay alive. I remember, when we came closer to the Ural Sea, the soldiers went out and bought salt, a huge sack of salt, and we did the same thing. Just two days' journey from that place, when we made stops, we had to take chances, the soldiers too. We began selling the salt, and within a day or so, we made up the money that we spent for that salt. After that, the rest was all profit, and with the profits we were able to buy other things. Our problem was that the train did not move much, and we stayed at the stations for longer periods than we traveled. The USSR, a mighty country, had only one rail, and whenever they had to bring transports from the opposite side, they pushed us aside at the station, and the other trains would come through. Only after a couple of days or so did they give us permission to move further. The journey was taking much longer than anticipated. The soldiers were also having difficulty with food, and the situation did not look good. I remember one evening, the soldiers decided to go out and get something. The rumors were that the transport that was standing in the station was carrying crates of chocolate, so the soldiers waited for nightfall, and then they went to work. They decided to go ahead and steal a crate and bring it to the car. They went ahead and after a while, they finally managed to steal a small crate. They brought it into the car, and we watched them open it. They were very happy, but not for long. When they finally broke the crate open, to their amazement, they brought in a crate of nails and not chocolate. They were cursing up and down because they had worked so hard and they only had nails to show for it.

As we slowly progressed on our journey, we were coming close to the city of Penza. And going to the city of Penza was uphill; there two locomotives pulled our transport rather than one, and this went on until we reached a suburb of Penza. When we reached the small station, our transport stopped in a deserted area, and we were positive that we would stand for a day or two if we were lucky, otherwise even longer, because we already knew the pattern. I asked the lieutenant if it was okay for me to go down to relieve myself under the wagon. He said, "No problem, go ahead." He opened the door—the door was really more or less half open or so—and I went down. As I went down and was about to go under the train to do what I had to do, I noticed a policeman in the distance. As soon as I saw him, I forgot that I had to relieve myself, and I went quickly back into the wagon, hoping that he did not see me. I informed the lieutenant that I saw a policeman but I did not know whether or not he saw me. The lieutenant closed the door, leaving just enough room for himself to stand in the door. He stood there with his machine gun swinging from his shoulder and looking out to see what was going on. We sat upstairs looking out of the window where we could see out but no one could see us. We saw this policeman approach and stop across from our train—there were other tracks, but he stayed on the tracks parallel to us and asked the lieutenant what a young boy was doing on a military train. The lieutenant, of course, denied the presence of any civilians aboard, and an argument ensued. The policeman demanded the right to enter the car. The lieutenant, knowing only too well what the consequences would be for himself, for his men, and for us, denied him permission, and the argument continued. At that very moment, the locomotive that had been attached to our train to pull it up the hill detached itself from us, switched rails, and started moving parallel to us on the same track the policeman was standing on. In the heat of their argument, the policeman neither saw the oncoming locomotive nor heard its three whistles signaling him to move off the track. The locomotive ran over the policeman, decapitating him, and the next thing we saw was his head rolling down the track. As if by a miracle our train began to move at that very moment. The lieutenant turned to us pale-faced and said, "*Eto vash Bog zdyela* (Your G-d did this), and we are safe." We were too stunned by this accident to either rejoice for ourselves or mourn for the policeman. When we arrived to the station in Penza, loudspeakers were broadcasting the news of the accident. We of course gave thanks to G-d for saving us and for making the train move at the same time that this happened. For days, we could not eat as a result of what we had witnessed. But it was this miracle that saved our lives and enabled us to continue with our escape out of Russia. When I close my eyes and think of this, I can still see that policeman, average height, a little bit on the heavy side. I can see before my eyes how his head rolled down and that blood was shooting out. For as long as I will live, I will never forget this incident, or should I say, this miracle. We all wondered, when we discussed this, whether our lieutenant saw the oncoming locomotive or if he too was so excited or frightened that he didn't see it. Because it is difficult to imagine, if the lieutenant saw the oncoming locomotive, why he didn't warn the policeman. That's something we always thought about, but we couldn't decide. Whatever it was, it saved our lives.

As we continued our journey, it got worse and worse. We finally reached Tambov, a large city that had a number of stores where we could obtain bread on our ration cards. So it was decided that my Aunt Rivka and I would go down with these cards, find a store, and get bread. We went down. I asked for directions to the store, because I spoke Russian and looked as Russian as any other Russian boy—nobody suspected that I was a foreigner. We finally got to the store; we received our bread and made our way back to the transport. Of course, we had to watch that nobody would notice that we were running to a military train. On the way back, we came to a pedestrian bridge, and I said to my aunt that she should walk on the lower level and I'd walk on the upper one and we'd meet on the other side. I was looking for a little bit of excitement. After all, I was only twelve years old. She did not object, so I walked up on the upper level; she was beneath, and when I crossed the bridge, I could not find my aunt. I began looking around, and then it dawned on me that we each went to a different place because the upper and lower levels of the bridge did not meet. I was looking and looking but I couldn't find her, and she, of course, looked for me too. She thought that I was going to make my way to the train, so she returned to the train. When she came back without me, she asked if I had already gotten back. They told her no and were completely stunned to see that she returned alone. She didn't know what to say. I, on the other hand, had backtracked and kept on looking for my aunt but couldn't find her. After a while, I decided to make my way to the train. As more time passed and my family didn't see me, my grandma fainted and my mother fainted; the military people began worrying not so much for me but that I might be picked up by the police and then give all this information. Meanwhile, I kept on looking for the train. Every transport had a number, and I remembered the number of ours. I did not approach the police; I knew what was involved even though I was so young, and somehow I finally managed to get to the place where the transport was. However, they had moved our train to a different location in that huge station, and my family was positive that they would never see me again. That entire time, I kept on running like a wild man between the tracks throughout the station searching and looking in each transport for our number train. At this time, my uncle went down from the train to look for me. My father went down from the train to look for me. The soldiers went down, and they too were going around searching and looking for me. And I ran around for about an hour and a half to two hours looking for the transport. I finally spotted the transport, G-d knows, kilometers away from where it was originally, and I began coming closer to the transport. That's when I noticed my uncle as well as one of the soldiers. And when they saw me from afar, they were the happiest people. At no time did anyone call out my name. I finally made my way to the transport without arousing any suspicion from the police or anyone else. No one stopped me; I did not approach anyone, and I finally made it back to the train. As luck would have it, I was on the train no more than five minutes when we started moving out of the station. In a city the size of Tambov, the train usually stayed for two or three days, and sometimes longer, but in this case, we stayed only from morning until late afternoon. If I had been five or ten minutes late, my family and I would never have seen each other again, and I would have been an orphan for the rest of my life. I would have cried for them, and they would have cried for me, and my aunt would have lived with a terrible conscience that she was responsible for losing me. But G-d was good to me; he watched over me, and I was safe. After this episode, the soldiers knew that they could trust me; my parents knew that they could trust me. Perhaps I should mention that I was the one who carried the money in a little pouch that they made and tied around my neck with a cord, because if adults were ever stopped, they would be searched, but children would not, especially a boy that looked so Russian. So the chances were better for me to get away with things than for them. They knew then that they could trust me. I had proven that. This was the third miracle. I had a life of miracles.

And so the journey continued. All in all, we traveled for seven weeks. The last two weeks were especially rough. The soldiers became very jittery, everybody was nervous, and food was running low. The bread cards were no good anymore—they had expired, and there wasn't much food for us or for the soldiers. The soldiers again were raiding other transports, looking for things. Sometimes they would be fortunate enough to find some things that they would sell; other times, they came up empty-handed, and the situation was not very good. The last week was really very bad. The lieutenant told us that he had received new orders, and he was not sure whether he could live up to the agreement that he made with us that he would deliver us to Poland, and we really did not know what to do. They really tried to dump us. But Vanya, when he was alone or outside with my father, he would just walk by and tell my father, "Don't pay any attention. Stay put, and don't listen." And we did just that. We stayed put for that week. We suffered. We only hoped that during the night, they would not throw us out someplace. We decided not to push our luck too much. When we came to the city of Kovel, Ukraine, even though it wasn't our destination, we decided to get off the train with the few things we had and hope for the best, because it was impossible to continue on that train. One of the reasons we decided to get off in Kovel was because my father knew the city very well. While serving in the Polish army, Father was stationed near Kovel, and so he always went there on his furloughs and for all the Jewish holidays. Whenever he was there for a holiday a different Jewish family invited him to stay with them, and in this way he got to know many families in the community over the two years. Kovel had a large, vibrant Jewish community. Jews lived in this city since 1536. The Jewish population in 1939 numbered approximately seventeen thousand out of thirty-three thousand people. Father figured that the city would be partially destroyed but would still have a number of Jews, and so we would somehow be able to manage. We arrived in the late afternoon, and when we got off the train, we saw that the station had been bombed out. We were in total shock to see the extent of the destruction. We lay there in the station, the entire family. We looked around and didn't know what to do. There was nothing to see except bombed-out areas. Then, we noticed a Russian soldier in the distance. To us, he somehow looked Jewish, and Father asked him what to do and explained the situation to him. The soldier was afraid to say too much to my father, but he did tell him that a number of times a week, there was a train leaving to Lemberg in the evening, and that in Lemberg there was a Jewish community. He also told us to be extremely careful because the previous night Poles killed a few Jews staying at the station. He warned us that we should do everything we possibly could not to remain at the station during the night, because something bad would happen. Then our dilemma was what to do and where to go. We were a family with children and Grandma. There was not much we could do. More and more people began gathering in the station by the tracks. Father saw a Polish colonel;

he saluted the colonel smartly, told him where he served, and asked for help. The colonel politely told Father that he couldn't be of help. Finally, we had no alternative but to spend the night at the station. None of us slept; we were on full alert. We hoped for the best, and, thank G-d, we survived the night without incident.

The next day my father decided to go into the city and look around—see what was going on. He hoped that maybe he would recognize someone or meet someone he knew. After all, he did know some people in this city while in the army. So again, he took me, and we walked into the city. We walked and we walked. Much of the city was bombed out. We walked on a street with very low buildings, mostly stores, and very few were damaged. There were very few people in the streets, and we continued walking. As we walked, a woman in her late twenties to early thirties walked by. As we walked past each other, my father turned his head and looked after her. She also turned and looked at my father. Then she slowed down. Then we slowed down. Finally, we stopped; she then walked back to us, and my father began talking to her. She recognized my father. She was a Jewish woman whose father used to do business with my father when they lived in Hrubieszow. They were in the wheat business, and Father had been in their house numerous times. She began to tell us a little bit about what happened with her and her family. She told us that she, her husband and children, as well as her parents were in the ghetto. She got to know a Polish man who was a member of the underground, and he tried to help her. He managed to smuggle her and her two children out of the ghetto, but when he went back again to smuggle her husband out, he did not succeed; the guards opened fire, killing her husband and badly wounding this Polish man. Her parents, too, died in the ghetto. After some time she married this Polish man who had rescued her and her two children from the ghetto, and they were living here in Kovel near the station. She told us also that there was no longer a Jewish community in Kovel and that most of the Jews congregated in Lemberg. She permitted us to come with our whole family and stay the night in her house with her family. When we heard that, we were in seventh heaven. But that's not all.

I mentioned earlier that there was a train that ran several times a week from Kovel to Lemberg (L'Vov). It was only a six- or seven-car train, depending on the evening, but there were thousands of people trying to get on it to be taken from Kovel to Lemberg. It so happened that her husband was the conductor of this train. Now I ask you, is there a G-d or isn't there a G-d? We were hopeful that something good would come out of this. The most important thing, of course, was that we would be safe because the family could stay at the woman's home. My father and I went to see where she lived, and then we hurried back to the station to take our family with the few possessions and go to her house. When we returned and told my uncle and the rest of the family what had happened, they had great difficulty believing what we said, but they knew it was true. We quickly picked up what we had and moved into the lady's house where we spent our second night in Kovel.

In the house, we met her husband, who was a very kind and polite individual. He told us he would arrange passes for us saying that we were wounded in the war, thereby having priority to board the train and sit in a designated wagon reserved for wounded. He did this knowing quite well that we had nothing to give him or pay him. We had no money, very little we could part with, and we had nothing left to give. Still, this Polish stranger did this for us because of his wife, and because he was a very decent person.

The next day, when we came to the station, we got there in the middle of the day. He told us where we should park ourselves, because he knew exactly where the train came to a stop, and he wanted us to be right where the designated wagon for the wounded stopped. We did as he told us, and when the evening approached, we realized the magnitude of his favor to us. The entire station was covered with people. It was an ocean of people. Thousands of people were gathering there, in the hopes of getting on the train to Lemberg. We were sitting on our spot there, and when the train pulled in, we presented our passes and got on the train. I wish it had been possible for me to obtain the address for this woman and gentleman. Not only would I send them a letter of thanks, but also I would help them with anything I could, because they truly saved our lives, and we had no way to thank them. All of this was done because this wonderful woman remembered my father coming to her home. Perhaps she did it for her father or for her father's memory. Wherever she and her husband and children are, I hope they are well.

Sixteen

It was when we arrived at Lemberg, later known as L'Vov, that the tragedy began to unfold more and more. We were directed to a synagogue, because that was where the Jews congregated. It seemed that all Jews who came to Lemberg stayed at the synagogue. You could still see that this huge synagogue was once magnificent. No one looked for privacy; we all stayed together on the floor. We found strength in numbers. The Germans used this synagogue for storage and stables. Many Jews were killed in this house of worship. We saw the places, and the reality of it began to sink in. We saw areas and graves where people were buried alive with body parts still sticking out. We began to see and realize what happened, but we still could not believe the reality of it.

Lemberg was an important Jewish center and had the third largest Jewish community in Poland. In 1939, it had 109,500 Jews, thirty-three percent of its total population. L'Vov had three Jewish secondary schools, a Hebrew college for advanced studies in Judaism, a nationalist religious school, Ma'ta't (Mi-Ziyyon Teze Torah), a vocational school, and many Talmud Torahs. There were many synagogues, and three Jewish newspapers were published.

The Jewish community in L'Vov was started in 1340 by Jews from Byzantium, Germany, and Bohemia. In September of 1939, at the start of World War II, L'Vov became part of the Soviet Ukraine. After the outbreak of the German-Soviet war, the Germans captured the city. That was July 1941, when it had a Jewish population of about one hundred fifty thousand, which included thousands of refugees from the Nazi-occupied western part of Poland. The Ukrainian population in the city welcomed the German troops, and Stefan Bandera, the leader of the Organization of Ukrainian Nationalists, and his units joined up with the Germans. They played a major role in stirring up hatred of the Jews and murdering them. They incited mobs that attacked the Jews for three days. Thousands of Jews were put in jail where they were tortured and murdered. During the same month, there was *Aktion Petliura*. *Aktion* was the name given to an official roundup of Jews, and Petliura was the name of a Ukrainian nationalist leader responsible for the pogroms that engulfed the Jews in the Ukraine during 1919 and 1920. *Aktion Petliura* was the name given to the premeditated mass murder of over two thousand Jews.

In March 1942, about fifteen thousand Jews from L'Vov were deported to Belzec Extermination Camp. However, the big *Aktion* took place from August 10–23, in which forty thousand Jews perished. Following the *Aktion*, the SS Gruppenfuehrer Fritz Katzmann ordered the establishment of a ghetto. When the Soviet forces entered in July 1944, there were 3,400 Jewish survivors, only 820 of whom were from the L'Vov ghetto itself.

Not much happened in Lemberg. I do remember there was a big marketplace not far from the synagogue. My father went to the marketplace and tried to do a little business there, buying and selling old clothing. Everything was done during the daylight. In the evening and night we avoided going out for fear of being killed.

My father became a very tense and nervous man. He saw what had happened but still could not accept the notion that he lost his entire family. He was positive in his heart that at least his brother, who was handsome, smart, and courageous, must have survived. And, it was pulling him to go closer and closer to our hometown. So we decided that we should try to reach Lublin. Lublin was our province, and we knew the area well. My father knew Lublin was a great Jewish center. It wasn't too far from L'Vov, and perhaps there, we'd be able to better see and hear what was going on. It was not so hard to move around then—we had very little to carry, in fact, practically nothing, and after about two weeks in L'Vov, we got on a train to Lublin.

My father remembered Lublin, the city of the *Maharam*, an acronym for *Moreinu Ha-Rav Meir* (our teacher, Rabbi Meir). He stemmed from Poland and was a highly respected Talmudist and *Halakhic* authority. Lublin was also the home of the renowned *Yeshiva Hakhme Lublin*. Father also remembered the attacks on the Jews of the city in the 1930s by the students of the Catholic University, whose rector was the author of anti-Semitic pamphlets. And he remembered the anti-Semitic propaganda in the city's leading Polish newspaper, *Glos Lubelski*—"Voice of Lublin." But despite all of this, the Jews in Lublin led an active social and cultural life with many schools, Zionist and anti-Zionist parties, and a Jewish Daily, *Lubliner Tugblat*. Before the war there were about forty thousand Jews in Lublin.

Seventeen

All this time I spoke Russian; I was already accustomed to it. Of course I knew Yiddish, but I was more comfortable speaking Russian. Even when my parents or grandmother spoke to me in Yiddish, I still answered in Russian. But for some reason, while on the train to Lublin, it just came out of my mouth—I started speaking Yiddish to my grandmother. The Poles were shocked when they heard me speak Yiddish. Perhaps they thought I was Russian or that all the Jews were dead, but once they heard me speak Yiddish, they showed their true colors. They started making preparations to throw me off the train—nothing more, nothing less. Of course my father watched out for me, but there were a lot of anti-Semites around us. Many Jews in Poland continued to be killed after the war. Luckily, we found a Russian soldier nearby, and my father gave him a bottle of vodka that he had bought in L'Vov. This was a valuable commodity, and as a result, this Russian soldier stood guard over me, literally, with his rifle, and watched and protected me until we arrived in Lublin. This was the welcome that I received from my countrymen, these born anti-Semites.

When we came to Lublin, it was again the same story. The city was partially bombed out. When we arrived at the station, we found out that very few Jews survived or lived in the city. Whatever Jews came, they all gathered in one place. The name of the place was *dom Peretza*, which means the house of Peretz, and the Jews were there because they felt more secure in larger numbers. But here too, the Jews had to watch themselves extremely carefully, because the Poles wanted to do them in. So we made our way to *dom Peretza*.

Lublin is right next door to Majdanek. And Majdanek, I do not have to describe. Everyone knows of this deadly place where thousands of Jews were murdered, including, I am sure, members of our family. We know of one family member who was definitely destroyed in Majdanek. He was my father's uncle's son, an only child, from the Brenner side of the family who lived in Hrubieszow. When his parents were taken to the ghetto, they managed to convince a Christian, a Polack, to hide their son. They paid the Polack a lot of gold for this, and after this couple was killed in the ghetto, the same Polack delivered the young man to the Nazis. He was shipped off to Majdanek, where he was killed.

We began to see things much more clearly in Lublin. We were hit with the reality that it would be extremely difficult, if not impossible, to find anyone from our family alive. I don't know whether my father was convinced that there were no survivors from his family; he never spoke of it, but he kept on hoping in his heart that maybe, just maybe, someone from the family would be found alive.

We saw where the ghetto was. We found out that the ghetto in Lublin was started up on April 24, 1941, with a population of about thirty-four thousand Jews. In March 1942, thirty thousand were deported to Belzec or murdered along the way. The remaining four thousand Jews were murdered between September and

October of the same year. The last two hundred survivors were sent to the Majdanek Death Camp. By July 24, 1944, when the Russian Red Army liberated Lublin, the city was practically *yuden-rein* (free of Jews). After its liberation, Lublin served as the temporary Polish capitol until 1945, at which time Warsaw was liberated. During that time Jewish organizations were established, one of them being "The Central Committee of Polish Jews." These organizations established *dom Peretza* and helped with whatever they could.

Anyway, once we were in Lublin, my father couldn't rest. It was sort of pulling him home. He was thinking that perhaps, if he could get down to Krylov, or to Ludmir, he could find out what happened. Maybe there was a chance that somebody did survive. If not his sisters or his brother, then maybe one of their children. Someone. With these thoughts in his mind, he went down to the railroad station in Lublin with Mother. They wanted to find out if there was a train and when the train would leave. And as they went down to the station, miraculously or fortunately, they met Shintovsky's daughter—our neighbor who was a very close friend of my mother's. I mentioned them earlier. This was the Christian family who spoke Yiddish fluently. This woman told my father about Krylov. First, she told him who became the chief of police (he was always an enemy of the Bichler family); then she told my father that if he showed his face into town, he would never come out alive. She also informed them of who took over the grocery store, the liquor store, the place where we used to keep the wheat, and who lived in our house, in my grandparents' house, uncle's and aunt's house. She told them everything about how the peasants there divided everything up amongst themselves, and she advised us that under no circumstances should we go to Krylov; in fact, we should stay as far away as possible. She also told them that there were no Jews at all in Krylov any more, and one Jew that my parents knew did come back, sold his house and field, and was killed after receiving the money. She herself didn't want to live in Krylov, because they killed her brother. She goes there just to visit her family. Hearing this, my father gave up the notion of going to Krylov or Ludmir, and we never set foot in our hometown again.

We continued living in Lublin, in *dom Peretza*. Every family was living in a little corner there. Each room had a number of families, a bed or so, and a number of people slept together in there. And somehow, we managed. It was just survival. We also found out that there were a number of Jewish families living in town, but it was very frightening and very insecure. I do remember that while we were in Lublin, the Russians were court-martialing a number of German officers who had high positions and were responsible for the slaughter of Jews and others at Majdanek. My parents, and many other adults, went to witness the executions at Majdanek, where they hanged them, but the children were not permitted to go. I also remember those who came back from there were in shock. They were telling of seeing fields with children's shoes, fields with ladies' shoes, fields with men's shoes, rooms with eyeglasses, rooms with human hair, as well as gas chambers and ashes of the murdered. It was not only difficult to talk about, it was difficult to listen. It was difficult to comprehend what took place there. For the first time, my parents were face-to-face with the cruel reality.

It was difficult to comprehend that these atrocities were thought up and committed by people who had wives, children, and parents; by G-d fearing people who went to church and who bowed and kissed the foot of Jesus, who was a Jew. How can a father of children take other little infants with their mothers and bury them alive? How can a human being make soap of men, women, and children? How can you incite your dog to rip a child to pieces while you watch with joy? The genocide was committed by devils in the shape of humans. Animals kill for food, or if they are in danger. But these human-looking beasts killed for pleasure. If there is such a thing as a Satan, he could not have thought up the atrocities that these lowest forms of human animals committed.

> "And cursed be the man who says: Avenge! No such revenge—revenge for the blood of a little child—has yet been devised by Satan."

> —Bialik
> "On the Slaughter"

Eighteen

Only months later we learned more or less what happened to father's family. We met Rachel, a very distant cousin of Mother's who survived in the ghetto of Vladimir Volinskiy (Ludmir) and later was in hiding. From her, we discovered that my father's sister Doba, her husband, and their three children never left Ludmir and ended up in the ghetto in town. The rest of Father's family did go to Kremenets. In Ludmir, when the Germans entered the city on June 25, 1941, there were twenty-five thousand Jews. On April 13, 1942, a ghetto was set up in two sections, one for skilled craftsmen, nicknamed by the Jews the "ghetto of life," and the second ghetto for the nonproductive, called the "ghetto of the dead." They contained altogether about twenty-two thousand Jews. On September 1, 1942, an *Aktion* began, lasting two weeks, in which eighteen thousand Jews were murdered: four thousand were killed in the prison courtyard and fourteen thousand in pits prepared in the Piatydni area. Doba and two of her children were there. They were sprayed with machine gun fire and then covered with earth while many were still alive. Her third child was ripped to pieces by a dog. Father never knew how his sister and her family died. We also found out from Rachel that my father's brother, Isaac, made it back to Vladimir Volinskiy.

What happened was that the Germans occupied Kremenets on June 22, 1941, at which time there were fifteen thousand Jews in town. In July of the same year, the Ukrainians, aided by Germans, killed eight hundred men, women, and children. Some of our relatives were probably among the eight hundred (we always heard rumors that many of our family were killed by Ukrainians). By March 1942, the ghetto was closed off from the rest of the city. The rest of our family must have been in the ghetto. On August 12, 1942, the Germans initiated a two-week-long *Aktion* to annihilate the inmates and then set the ghetto ablaze to drive out those in hiding. That must have been when the rest of the family was killed and Father's brother Isaac escaped to Ludmir. The vast majority of the ghetto inhabitants rounded up in the *Aktion* were taken in groups and murdered over trenches dug near the railway station. Only fourteen of the Kremenets community survived the Holocaust. Isaac, the only survivor of the family in Kremenets, made it back to Ludmir. According to Rachel, he was hidden in a bunker with the *shochet* of our town and some others. Only one week before the Russians freed the city, July 22, 1944, was the hiding place discovered and raided. Isaac escaped but was shot by a Ukrainian. Only a few dozen Jews, out of twenty-five thousand, were found alive at liberation.

We continued staying in Lublin for a number of weeks. Then my family decided that there was no future there, that we must move to an area where there was a greater Jewish community and perhaps more opportunity for a better livelihood. The Jews from the villages and *shtetlach* (relatively small communities) ended up in the concentration camps, and those who survived the war knew they'd be killed if they tried to return. We heard that Jews were congregating in Lodz, a very large city in central Poland that was the center of the textile industry before the war. At the outbreak of World War II, Lodz had two hundred thirty-three thousand Jews. When the Soviets liberated Lodz on January 19, 1945, 870 Jews were left in the city. Nevertheless, within a short period of time, Lodz became a large reconstructed Jewish community. We packed up the few things we had and began making our way to Lodz. On the way, we stopped at a number of stations, and at times the train would remain in the station for up to an hour if not more. At one stop, I do not remember the name of the town, my Aunt Rivka went to the bathroom. Within minutes, she was back, pale-faced and crying. We all looked at her and thought that someone attacked her. It would not have been surprising. However, it turned out that she saw a woman stand next to her in the washroom, and she thought it was her sister Frumke. She tried to approach her, but the woman ignored her. She was certain that her sister was rejecting her for running away from home in 1939. We all looked at her in disbelief. Mother and Grandma decided to go with her to see the woman. They saw the young woman outside the bathroom, and she did resemble Frumke. Once they engaged her in conversation, they were convinced she was not Frumke, but Rivka kept on crying. Months later, we found out the truth about beautiful Frumke. She married while we were in Siberia. When the Germans began rounding up and killing Jews, she ran back to her village of Dalobechif to a farmer she knew. Apart from hiding her, the son of the farmer kept on raping her. She became pregnant, and when she could not hide her pregnancy any more, the farmer's son murdered her. Aunt Rivka knew the farmer well.

After the war, people who survived searched high and low for their wives, husbands, parents, children, and any other members of their families. Very few were fortunate enough to find someone alive; the great majority was unfortunate. As if this were not enough, some survivors underwent other traumatic experiences.

Braindl, my uncle's sister-in-law, the one who went to the *kolkhoz* when she was pregnant, got married to a man who survived the camps. He had witnesses who saw his wife on line to the gas chambers. The rabbi spoke to the witnesses and married them. After a few months, Braindl became pregnant. Miraculously, after the good news, the man's first wife appeared alive and well. The man was very happy, delighted, excited, and confused. Not knowing what to do, he ran to the rabbi for advice. The rabbi ruled that, being Braindl was pregnant, he should divorce his first wife and remain with Braindl. Such was life for some survivors, tragedy after tragedy.

In Lodz, a number of Jewish institutions were already functioning. One of them directed us to a little house where the Jewish ghetto was. We moved in there. Everything around us was destroyed. Only parts of houses were standing. It looked more like a cemetery with headstones than a place for people to live. There was not a living soul around us, when I think back. I just can't comprehend how we went in there, with children, to stay in that house, and not think about the consequences. Somehow, somebody watched over us.

Lodz was severely damaged, especially the area of the Jewish ghetto. Some parts of the city remained intact, and they were quite beautiful. Fortunately for us, we did not stay too long in that little house. My father went into the marketplace to see what he could do, and he again began buying and selling old clothing. While there, he met his cousin Meir Kuperman. If you remember, his brother was the one whom the Jewish Communists shot, and this was the only survivor that my father found from his mighty family. He was selling clothing and all kinds of things at the market; he immediately gave my father certain things to sell. My father began selling, and within a short period of time, he began earning money there, and we were able to support the family. Meir Kuperman got married in Lodz to a young lady who was a survivor of the ghetto.

She was born and lived in Lodz all the time. She had an apartment, and the apartment was standing empty, so they gave us the apartment and urged us to move out of our little house immediately. The apartment was on Kamyena; it was not a very good neighborhood, but it was much, much better than the burned-out ghetto. This area was a red light district, and whenever you walked there, you could hear from the windows the young ladies shouting prices for their services. Nevertheless, the place was much better than what we had. We still felt very insecure because there were very few Jews in the area. However, by then (1946), more Jews began coming into the city. The Soviet Union opened its doors and permitted the Polish Jews to return "home" legally. They came by the thousands to Lodz. Whenever we learned of a family from Krylov coming, we took them into our apartment. We ended up being five families in a three-room apartment. We felt more secure, especially at night; there were many more people to protect ourselves against the Poles.

With thousands of Jews in the city, the number of Jewish institutions increased. A Jewish theater as well as a Jewish public school was established. A number of Jewish papers (Yiddish, Hebrew, and Polish language) appeared. Zionist organizations conducted activities with the support of the majority of Jews. A number of *kibbutzim* (homes for Jewish youth who prepared themselves for immigration to Palestine) were established. The children of our family as well as those of the other families, with the exception of my baby sister Chaya, did not remain home very long. The parents inquired about education for the children and found out that there were such things as kibbutzim there, and if you handed over the children to the kibbutz, they would protect them, feed them, educate them, and care for them. So, we all went to the same kibbutz. It was the kibbutz Dror, a Zionistic kibbutz. It was almost like a home, more like an orphanage than a kibbutz. But the idea was that they promised they would take us out of Poland to Germany, and from Germany eventually to Palestine. The children AND the parents. And of course, this was what we hoped for, because we saw that there was no future on the bloody soil of Poland. In the beginning, we were all in a kibbutz on Zachodna Street—I believe #16— where the children and the adults were all in the same building but in separate rooms. The rooms were huge, and there were many beds in the rooms. In my bed, we were four children. The children in the kibbutz were from many different backgrounds. Some children came from the forests, some came from Russia as my family and I did, and others were orphans who came from ghettos and hiding places. Some of these children were very, very wild, and we all had to live together. Day and night, the adults guarded us because they feared attacks by the Poles. Life in that kibbutz from the beginning was quite frightening. We were about fifty kids divided up into a few very large rooms with a stove in the middle of each room. The undisciplined ones played harmful tricks on the rest of us, and we had to be very careful and on a constant lookout. For example, when we went to sleep, those kids would get up in the middle of the night and take paper, put it between the toes of the unsuspecting sleeping kids, and set the paper on fire just for fun. Another favorite of theirs was to take metal cups, heat them up on the stove, and put them on children's cheeks, leaving their faces scarred for life. Sometimes they poured cold water on the kids in the middle of the night even though it was wintertime and freezing cold. They did numerous other things as well. They were very creative. In order to survive, what my group of four did was take turns keeping guard from our bed. Every couple of hours, we would rotate and take turns sleeping. This way, we made sure that nothing happened to the four of us in the bed. It was truly survival of the fittest.

After living in this place for four or five weeks, a number of troublemakers were thrown out. We moved out to a place that was just a children's kibbutz. It was a very beautiful place. It was a magnificent villa on Vilchaynska Street, #78. It belonged to a Jewish millionaire in the textile business. He was the only survivor of his family, and he turned over his mansion to the kibbutz and took only one small room for himself. We were about fifty youths, and it was so huge that we were quite comfortable in it. Each child had his own cot, and there was sufficient room for all of us. The dining room had two or three huge chandeliers and a very big table that made it possible for all the children to sit around it and eat together. Once we moved to Vilchaynska #78, life became much nicer and more normal. All the children were registered to a school; we had a Hebrew school, and there was one period a day where they taught us Polish. But in Polish class, we didn't pay too much attention. I remember I and my other friends used to cut that class many times. The school was, of course, for all the Jewish students in Lodz, and we had quite a number there. I do not recall how many, but I remember that some older ones came to the school and some carried guns. I still remember one boy very vividly—he was older and carried around a gun, which he would show us. Perhaps he needed it for his survival, I do not know. When we got home from the school, our *madrichot* (counselors) would help us with our homework. It was almost mandatory to sit down and do the homework. That was the first thing, and as I mentioned, the *madrichot* would walk around and help anyone who needed help. The *madrichot* were wonderful young ladies. Their names were Chaya, Esther, and Dorka. Esther was in the kibbutz with her elderly mother. Weeks later, a fourth *madricha* joined; she was from Palestine, from kibbutz Yagur. I can't remember her name. Life at the kibbutz wasn't bad at all. It was quite good, as a matter of fact. We received three decent meals a day. We received half-decent clothing. And we also received a little culture. We were taught Israeli songs, Israeli dances, and a little bit of Jewish history, Zionism. And when the Israeli *madricha* came, we began hearing stories from Palestine about life in the kibbutz, all kinds of things. And listening to these stories was very pleasant. Sometimes our imaginations would run away with us. On Fridays, after school, everybody began making preparations for the *oneg Shabbat*, a Friday night party in honor of the Sabbath. We sang songs, listened to the reading of stories, ate cake or cookies, and drank soda. They gave each child a clean shirt and clean underwear for Shabbat. If they liked you, they gave you a nicer shirt. They happened to have liked me. Chaya used to call me *"Avreimele melamed"* and used to pick out a nicer shirt for me. Maybe it's because she also liked my sister a lot. I used to look forward to the *oneg Shabbat*. First of all, the food was a little bit better. We had all kinds of skits put together by Chaya, who was extremely bright. She wrote poems; she wrote songs and added certain melodies to them. She came up with all kinds of things. And then of course we had group singing, and they taught us Hebrew songs. We learned to dance the hora among other things, and other dances. It was quite lively and very, very pleasant. After a number of weeks at the kibbutz, we also learned the *techezakna*, the workingman's national anthem in Palestine. And every night, before we would go to sleep, the entire group of children would line up in two lines, stand at attention, sing the *techezakna*, and then a few announcements would be made for the following day. Then they would read the names of the people who would have to stand guard and at what time they would have to stand guard, and finally, we went off to sleep. Fear wasn't totally gone because we were not secure. No Jew was secure in Poland. And every night, we used to have two young men, and sometimes girls too, who would come from the adult kibbutz to stand guard over us at night, in case of an attack. Most of the time, young ladies from the adult kibbutz would be the ones to carry weapons, small guns, in their brassieres because they would be less suspicious in case they were stopped in the streets or searched. They would bring the weapons, and then they would return to their kibbutz, and the two young men would remain standing guard over us. With them, there were always a boy and a girl from our kibbutz who were also on guard duty. And every few hours, we changed off, and the adults also changed off. Seldom did we go off by ourselves because it was very dangerous. When we did go, it was always in groups, and we never played in the streets. We did have a backyard that came with the house, and in the backyard, we played only during the day and always under supervision because of the danger from some of the Polish people. Our group of boys and girls were very peculiar, sometimes strange and sometimes heroic. We had all kinds of people.

One boy that comes to mind is Leon. He was a little bit older than the others. Nice-looking boy, black curly hair, quite tall. He and his brother tried to escape from the ghetto in Warsaw by jumping over the wall. It seems like his brother was killed there, or so he thought because his brother did not move, so he left him there and ran. Somehow, he managed to escape out of the city to a Polish farmer who hid him until the end of the war. It was not so easy to hide a boy; a girl was much easier. But obviously this man, this Polish man, must have been a wonderful person. After the war, this same wonderful man took this boy and brought him to a Jewish organization, and somehow from the Jewish organization, this boy ended up in our kibbutz.

Another boy that comes to mind was a very close friend of mine. His name was Yisroel Litmanovich, and he was there with an older brother, Ze'ev. They survived in the forest; they were partisans. As a matter of fact, their father was killed there. This boy was limping a little bit, and it was especially noticeable when he tried to run. He had great difficulty. Yisroel told me the reason for it. When they were in the forest, many times they would dig huge holes, like caves. They would cover the tops with branches and all kinds of wood for camouflage so the Nazis wouldn't notice them. One day, as he was sleeping in one of those holes, the news spread very quickly that the Nazis were about to raid the area. They all ran away, and in the great panic, his mother, brother, and the others there forgot about him, and he remained sleeping in that hole. When he woke up, he heard people walking on top of him. He realized they were Germans; he kept on lying in that cave, and he remained there for some days. Luck was with him—the Germans didn't find him and after a few days, his mother and the others returned to find him alive and well. However, he paid a price for it. His toes froze off, and therefore, he was unable to run or walk like the rest of us.

There was another young man there, who often behaved very cruelly. He didn't care very much when he saw people suffering. We later learned that he had been hidden, with his family, in some kind of a bunker. His mother was holding his baby sister, who began crying. When they heard the Nazis marching around and walking above them, the other people in their bunker told her to make sure the baby didn't cry. The mother put a hand on the little baby's mouth, but she was so frightened herself that she didn't realize that her hand not only covered the girl's mouth, but also her nose. When the Nazis moved away and the danger passed, they realized the baby girl was dead. We all thought this terrible episode had a very negative influence on this young man.

We had other kids who were very peculiar, and when I look back now, I realize they were really mentally ill. We had kids who were afraid to go to the bathroom at night, so when they got up in the middle of the night, they would go over to somebody's boots and urinate into their boots or shoes, then quickly go back to sleep as if nothing had happened. And then when we got up in the morning one of us would generally find his shoe or boot wet and foul smelling as he put his foot into it. Since we had no other shoes to wear, whatever the boy did in the shoe had to be dealt with because we had no choice but to continue to wear our shoes. Because of these occurrences, we always had to sleep with one eye open to watch and be on guard. It was always survival of the fittest. We tried to catch these kids, and we made arrangements with the boys who stood on guard duty to help us. Every once in a while we caught the person who did this. We were always amazed at how normal that person's behavior was during the day, but somehow at night, something went wrong and the boy just couldn't help himself because of his fears. It was difficult for us to understand because there were always people there on guard, yet he was afraid to go to the bathroom, and there wasn't much we were able to do about it. We never beat him, because it was against the law. We would inform the *madrichot*, and the *madrichot* would try to talk to him, but we still had to keep our eyes open.

In this kibbutz in Lodz, we stayed for a number of months, maybe four or five months, maybe even more, I cannot recall exactly. Every once in a while, we would go to visit our parents, but never alone. At certain times, our parents came to visit us. The parents, I must say, were very happy that we were in the kibbutz because they did not have to worry about feeding us or educating us, and more than that, about protecting us from what was going on in the streets. With all the protection we had, we still had to be extremely careful.

A boy, Chaim, who was from our town and his family lived in my family's apartment, was with us in the kibbutz. The kibbutz bought a bicycle and Chaim, being one of the oldest and a so-called leader of this kibbutz, took the bicycle and went for a ride in the streets. A Polish young man came over to him, knocked him off the bike, and tried to take the bike away. He put up a little fight, and during that fight, he was stabbed and the bike was taken away. When the police came, they threw Chaim in jail. Fortunately for him, the stab wound wasn't too deep, and he survived. He was in jail for about a day or two until the kibbutz leaders found out, went to the jail, got him out, and brought him back to the kibbutz.

In Lodz we heard all kinds of rumors about kidnapping Jewish children, killing them, and making salami out of them. It may sound strange, but it was believable because when we traveled from L'Vov to Lublin—I did not mention this previously—and we came to the city of Przemysl, we spent the night at the station waiting for a connecting train to Lublin in the morning. We were about six families. The Poles came around looking at us, and they were shocked to see so many Jews still alive. They began looking at us and shouting at us that they will make *myensa* (meat) out of us. There's not much difference between meat and salami. We were so frightened that I remember my father and a few other men went to look for the Russian authorities. When they found them and told the Russians the story, they sent a patrol to guard us at the station at night so those wonderful Poles would not be able to fulfill their desire.

But going back to Chaim, he was stabbed, his bike was taken away, and yet he was thrown in jail. This was Poland, and mind you, this was after World War II and not during the war. When we went to our parents' house, we had to be very careful. The neighborhood they lived in was not a very good one—it was a red light district area, and you passed by houses with many apartments used for prostitution that attracted criminal and underworld figures. You had to be extremely careful when you walked around that area. I remember one famous slogan there that the pimps used to shout from their windows: "*Kamiena*, five for twenty-five." For twenty-five zlotys, you were able to get the girl. It was especially very dangerous to walk there at night. I remember once, my father had a close encounter with disaster. He took down the garbage one evening, and as he was walking with the garbage to the yard, a man next to him walked by carrying a small attaché case. From out of nowhere, another man jumped out, shot the man with the attaché case to death, grabbed the attaché case, and ran away. This happened right in front of my father's eyes. My father was fortunate that he himself wasn't shot that time. After that incident, he never took the garbage down in the evening. If he had to do something, it was done during daylight hours only.

To see people die there was a normal occurrence. You would see it practically every day. I remember once walking on the main street, called *Marshalkovska*, and there were buildings that were damaged. Polish authorities used to use Germans, like slave labor, to rebuild these buildings. There were people standing and working on the fifth or sixth floor, and one of the workers fell down and hit the sidewalk. He was lying there and bleeding, and people just walked by as though nothing had happened. They didn't even pay attention to the guy. Maybe it was because he was German, or maybe it was just part of everyday life.

We also had other problems. The Polish went back to their old tricks. They began making pogroms, and I remember our entire kibbutz went to a funeral together with practically all the other Jews who lived in Lodz. What happened was a number of boys and girls who belonged to a religious kibbutz were on a truck someplace outside of Lodz. They were ambushed and killed. And the only reason why they were killed was because they were Jews. The Poles began showing their true colors. It would be safe to say that Poles killed hundreds, if not thousands, of Jews after World War II. Some of them killed the Jews because of hate. Others, from the small towns where the Jews returned after the war, killed them so they wouldn't have to return the homes or the stores or whatever else they seized from the Jews. And still others, perhaps fearing that the Jews might know something or testify against them, killed Jews as well. *Shoah*, a film about the Holocaust made by a Frenchman, bears out what I am saying here.

We should remember that the Polish people made a very large pogrom in Kielce after the war. Kielce, in 1939, had about twenty-five thousand Jews. After the war, about two hundred Jews were in Kielce. Some were survivors of Nazi camps or hidden in the district, and others had come back from the Soviet Union. Their reconstruction of the former organized Jewish community aroused anger among Polish anti-Semites. They began a campaign against the existence of a renewed Jewish community in the city. The campaign culminated in an armed pogrom against the Jews (July 4, 1946). The Jews had no adequate means for self-defense since the police had confiscated the few pistols from them just one day prior. In this pogrom, forty-two Jews were murdered, and many others wounded. The pogrom gave impetus to the Jewish survivors in Poland and those who returned from the Soviet Union to leave this bloody, cursed land for the West.

Lodz and Kielce were only two of the places where Jews were murdered. In many, many places in Poland, Jews were killed. No place in Poland after the war was safe for Jews. You had to be alert and on guard twenty-four hours a day in order to survive.

While we were in the kibbutz in Lodz, very distinguished visitors honored us. The couple that came was none other than Zivia Lubetkin and Yitzhak Zuckerman. They were leaders, fighters, and survivors of the Warsaw Ghetto Uprising. They were true heroes. Zivia spent about two weeks in our kibbutz, while Yitzhak only a number of days. Perhaps the war was a little too fresh in our minds; we could not truly appreciate the importance of Zivia and Yitzchak. They came to stay with Dorka before leaving for Palestine. They were permitted to settle in Palestine legally by the

British authorities. They were very close friends of Dorka's. They fought and suffered together for many years.

Life at the kibbutz was pretty good. They tried to do whatever they could, physically and spiritually, for us. They tried to instill in us love for the Land of Israel, Zionism, to bring us as close as possible to Palestine. I even remember, on *Tu B'Shvat* (Arbor Day, when in Israel, they plant thousands of trees, and outside of Israel, we send money to Israel to plant trees and we eat fruits from the Holy Land), *shlichim* (emissaries) from Palestine came and brought us oranges from the Land of Israel. That was something extraordinary. We heard stories about the Land of Israel, and they taught us the latest dances and songs. We did not know the meaning of the songs, but we knew them all by heart, and we did all the dances, and it was quite pleasant and very interesting. When a *shaliach* (emissary) would come and speak to us about the Land of Israel, we looked on him not as a regular human being, but as a superman, an angel dropping in. We would not only look, we wanted to touch the person. Wow! He came from Palestine; he came from the Land of Israel! He must be great! This was the feeling that we had, and they built up in us this feeling of love for the Land of Israel, pride, and a desire to go there as soon as possible. We heard so many stories about the kibbutzim D'ganya, Ein Charot, Yagur, and others that we felt as if we knew every place and were part of what was happening in those places. Once in a while, we even got to see pictures of the kibbutzim and the children on them. Everyone knows a picture is worth a thousand words, and we used to eat this up. We were looking forward, hoping and dreaming of the day when we could be a part of it.

Nineteen

We stayed in Lodz until the middle of April 1946. The promise the leaders of the kibbutz movement made to the parents when they registered us in the kibbutz, was kept. They began making arrangements with the *Brichah* to take us out of Poland to Germany and of course, eventually, to Palestine. They were not only going to take us out, but also our parents. The *Brichah* was the name of an organized underground operation that moved Jews out of Poland and other eastern European countries to central and southern Europe between 1944 and 1948, as a step toward their "illegal" immigration to Palestine. Groups of Jewish partisans, remnants of Warsaw Ghetto fighters, and Zionist groups returning from Soviet Asia under the leadership of Abba Kovner formed the *Brichah*. They worked together with the Jewish Brigade and representatives of Palestine, who exercised control over *Brichah* activities.

All the parents were informed of the steps that were being taken. They were told to be in contact and to be ready to move on a moment's notice. We, the children, were moved first. We packed everything we had—of course, we did not have very much. When we were on the go many times, if we had two pairs of pants, we put on both pairs. If we had more than one shirt, we'd put those on, too. The premise was that if you were wearing it, it was safe. But if you carried these things, chances were pretty good that they would get lost, or somehow disappear. We made our way to the train station and boarded the train to Stettin, a German city that was then part of Poland.

When we got on the train, it was packed with people. I remember, I got myself a spot above a door. There was a metal railing that was about an inch and a half in diameter, and somehow I got up and sat on top of that for hours. Even today, I cannot see how it was possible for me to sit all the way up for so many hours on that thin railing. As I mentioned before, we traveled separately from our parents. I do not know whether my parents also had to take a train to Stettin, or whether they traveled by trucks. But I do know that after a few days they, too, made it to Stettin, because I remember seeing my parents there once. In Stettin, we stayed in a house. I don't remember much about this house, but I do remember quite well that the city was very badly damaged by the bombs. It was a port city, and quite a bit of it was destroyed. I also remember that we did not have much of anything in the house we were in. Not even enough dishes for us to eat from, and not too many chairs or tables. We had very little in there because it was a temporary place for us. So a few of the boys and I—maybe three or four other boys—hung out together. Of course there was no school or anything of that sort. We just roamed around in that area. We used to go into bombed-out houses—some of these houses were halfway bombed out—and somehow we never worried about anything and we never thought about anything. We just crawled around looking for things. We were not particular. We looked for anything and everything. We looked for chairs, a table, clothing, and dishes;

anything that would be useful, we looked for, and if we found it, we would bring it back to the kibbutz.

One day, while we were roaming through these half-destroyed houses, not thinking of any danger, we got into a house that was partially damaged, and it was practically across the street from a police station in the city. The house was about three or four stories high, I cannot recall. We were four boys, and the entire house was filled with crates. We walked through every floor; we looked at these crates and finally decided to break the crates open. We started with one. We broke it open and found that it contained German money. We broke open another one—more money. We broke open crates on each floor, and every crate we opened was filled with German money. It was German money that was from before World War II, and we thought that because Germany lost the war, the money was not good. But the truth of the matter was that the money was good. It wasn't worth THAT much, but it was still worth quite a bit. It was DM 200 to US $1. At that time, my parents had nothing. And here I was, sitting on a house full of money, and we didn't pay much attention to it. We used the money for toilet paper there and didn't bring anything to the kibbutz. We were in that building a number of times. Once I took two DM 50 bills. I put them in my pocket as a souvenir and didn't mention it to anyone. The other boys didn't take anything. And somehow no one, not a single one of us, ever mentioned the episode of finding this money to any adult or to any *madrich* or *madricha* in the kibbutz; we just ignored it.

After being in Stettin about two weeks, preparations were made for us to leave. Of course everything was done illegally. The kids from our kibbutz were divided into two groups. A two-door armored truck was brought in for us. At the bottom of the truck was a little trap door, so to speak; it may have been an emergency exit. We were able to get into that armored truck only by the side door. In the front there was the driver, and next to him was a *Brichah* man with a machine gun; inside the truck we were about twenty-five children. This truck was a bit peculiar. Inside, it was very dark, and the only light we had came from the driver's window. There were beams running through the length or width of the truck, and if you raised your head a little too high, you were smacked by one of those beams, which was extremely painful. Next to me was sitting a boy by the name of Itche Bitterman. His parents lived in our apartment in Lodz; we called him "*Itchale*," in a mocking way. He was about six feet tall, and in those days that was very, very tall. Somehow, he received a new pair of boots from his parents, and every time I touched his boot, he would try to hit me and I would try to move my head away. Every time I moved my head, I kept forgetting about these beams, and I would smack my head against the beams—it was quite painful. I wasn't the only one that he tried to hit. He did the same with the others around him, and we all had a very painful journey. Now, we were in this truck for quite a while, and as we were riding, we were approaching the border between Poland and Germany. I was quite near to the driver and the side of the trap door, so I was able to see what was going on. The *Brichah* man jumped out with his machine gun, and the border police raised their hands and threw their rifles down; he gave them a bag full of money, then he jumped back into the truck, and the truck took off very fast. They did not fire any shots. It seems they were happy with the gift they got from this young fellow with the machine gun, and they did not bother firing after us. The truck was moving, and as we were speeding, a terrible tragedy almost happened. Suddenly the trap door opened halfway. Chaim, another boy from my town, began falling out. We all started screaming. Fortunately for him, and for all of us, I on one side and another boy on the other side grabbed him and pulled him back in. The driver slowed the truck down, and we closed the door. How fortunate Chaim was. He could have easily lost his life. Today, Chaim lives in Tel Aviv. I saw his mother in 1956, during my first trip to Israel, but I didn't see Chaim. He was embarrassed to come and see me, but I never learned why.

We came into the middle of a forest, and the truck stopped. There was a little house that we went into, and we stayed there. It was more like a shack. There was nothing inside. We all slept on the floor and ate mostly bread. It was a *Brichah* station. We stayed there, waiting for the other members of our kibbutz to come and join us. We were in that place about three days until the other group met up with us. While there, we were not allowed to wander off. We were told to either stay in the shack or right next to it if we went out. We had to lay low; it was the Russian zone. After about three days there, we dressed up more or less with our things and sort of looked like students on a hike. We were told not to speak, not to make too much noise, just to march. We walked for quite a while, and after a couple of hours we came to a place where there was a restaurant or beer garden. They told us they would take us in to have a drink, some lemonade, and we should try to keep quiet. We all went in there, and after resting for a while we drank something. It was still East German territory. One of the *Brichah* guides took some money out to pay the bill, and I noticed that he was paying with the same money that I found in that house in Stettin. I pulled out my DM 50 bill and showed it to him. He called me over to the side, and he said to me, "Where did you get this money?" I decided I might as well tell him the entire story. I explained to him where the building was, and I told him that this building contained crates of German money, that we broke open a great number of these crates on each of the floors, and that every one of them was filled with money in DM 50 denominations. He looked at me not knowing what to say. He asked me again some questions about it, and again I explained everything to him. It was difficult for him to believe what I was telling him, but I believe eventually he was convinced that I was sincere about this. And again he asked me about the location, and again I explained to him where it was. I am sure that this young man did not take the money for himself. I am sure that this man, who belonged to the *Brichah*, put the money to very good use. I only hope they took all of this money, because the *Brichah's* money went for smuggling Jews out of Poland and Eastern Europe to Palestine by way of Germany and other countries. I always wondered what would have been had I told my father about this money. If I would have only shown him a DM 50 bill when I saw him in Stettin. We probably would not have had to crawl on our bellies in the forests, suffering so much. We probably would have gone out in style and helped G-d knows how many more people to get out without suffering. Perhaps my parents would not have had to work so hard to support our family for the rest of their lives. But it was not to happen. On the other hand, I was always very proud that I was able to make such a contribution to the *Brichah*. It made me feel a part of them. I cannot imagine them not coming back to me if the money had not been found. I always hoped that this great fortune did not go into the pockets of private individuals.

We finally came to the French zone in Berlin. Once we came to the French zone it was much better. We ate decent food and had a place to sleep. We stayed in Berlin maybe a week. No more than that. We were excited to be in Berlin. We had heard quite a bit about the city. But we saw nothing except destruction, and we were not sorry.

From the French zone we were taken to a train station where we boarded a train for Munich. From Munich trucks took us to a Displaced Persons (DP) Camp by the name of Leipheim. The term Displaced Persons was used to describe people who were driven out of their homes as a result of Nazi decrees during World War II. At the end of the war there were approximately eight million Displaced Persons in Germany and Nazi-occupied territories. The Allied powers rapidly solved the DP problem by repatriating most of the DPs back to their homes. The remainder, which consisted of those who would not or could not be repatriated for political reasons, were put into special camps under the auspices of the United Nations Relief and Rehabilitation Administration (UNRRA).

The Jewish DPs presented a problem of a different nature. Most of the Jewish survivors came to realize that they had no place to return to since their families were no longer alive and their communities were destroyed. Jewish survivors began making their way to DP Camps in Germany in the hope of being recognized by the Allies as a separate category of refugees. Their purpose was to be rehabilitated in a new homeland rather than to be included in the groups of refugees according to their country of origin.

Our trip to Leipheim was very interesting. It took about three hours. We displayed Jewish flags and sang Hebrew songs as we were driving through Bavaria, Hitler's base of support. But in Poland, our homeland for hundreds and hundreds of years, we were afraid to walk in the streets. It was rather ironic. Once we arrived to the DP Camp, our kibbutz was set up in Barrack #9.

Within a little more than a week, our parents arrived to the same camp, and they were set up in Barrack #6. When we arrived to Leipheim, it was Lag B'Omer, the thirty-third day of the counting of the Omer, which is reckoned from the second day of Passover until Pentecost (Shavuot). It occurs on the eighteenth day of the Hebrew month of Iyar and has been celebrated as a semi-holiday since the ninth century. On Lag B'Omer, the traditional mourning customs of abstention kept during the Omer period are lifted. Marriages, celebrations, and entertainment are permitted. I will always remember May 19, 1946. We stayed perhaps for an hour or two in the barrack, and then we all went out to the soccer field, right across from our barrack, to celebrate Lag B'Omer. We all walked around as if in a daze. It looked the way we envisioned Israel, but a small version of it. We had not seen so many friendly faces in a very long time. We got chocolates and fruits and lots of other goodies. The kids were playing games; we were looking all around and didn't know where to look first. There were hundreds and hundreds of people. I think the entire camp population must have been at this sports field. What a change! The day before, and the day before that, we were in the forest hiding and moving quietly through all kinds of dangers. Then suddenly, we were in Little Israel. Unbelievable. Unbelievable. We were homeless and stateless, but we were free and without fear.

Twenty

Leipheim itself was a very scenic, beautiful town in Bavaria. It sat on the Dunhau River surrounded by fields, orchards, gardens, and forests. It was absolutely magnificent. One hour away, we had Augsburg, and not far from us was also Ulm. Munich was two hours away by train. In the camp, we were about twenty-five hundred Jewish people, and we were situated in a very beautiful area. There were fields and woods around the camp, and about three or four miles away was the beautiful Dunhau River. About a mile away from the camp was a huge airfield. It had once been a *messerschmidt* base, and the barracks were used to house the pilots and others who maintained the base. All around the airfield one could see bombed-out planes and bombed-out hangars. Everything around the field that had to do with the military was bombed out. But the airfield and the camp itself were in perfect condition. The airfield ran from Leipheim to Ginsburg, I would say at least five to six kilometers. In the camp, there were many, many barracks. It was a very huge complex, and this entire complex was turned into a Displaced Persons Camp.

Life in camp became much more normal. We had a Hebrew School; we had other activities; we were able to walk around and do anything we pleased. We played soccer. We did everything. It was not like in Poland. For the first time we felt like free human beings. The kibbutz itself was different from the kibbutz in Lodz. It became more like a military unit. We were four boys in one room. There were two bunk beds to a room, and each boy had a bed. And practically at all times, whatever we did, we did together, the entire kibbutz. In the morning, everyone had to get up at about six o'clock. The older kids were in charge; they would run through, throwing everyone out of the bed, and we would have to exercise or run for a couple of kilometers. Then we would come back, wash, brush our teeth, take our books, and march to a kitchen where we would eat breakfast. Every morning, as we marched, we sang Hebrew songs just like in Israel. We marched very smartly, and everyone in the camp used to look out and admire the way we sang and marched. We were sort of like the alarm clock for many people in camp. And after we ate breakfast in the public kitchen, we marched to the school. Everywhere was marching, but from school, we did not march. From there, we came back to the kibbutz at our leisure. We had to do our homework, and after we were done with our homework, we would go outside and play soccer for a number of hours. Afterwards, we would come back to the kibbutz, and of course, again, march to eat dinner. Then in the evening, we would line up and stand at attention while we sang the *techezakna*. The announcements for the following day would then be read, and only then could we go off to bed. On Fridays, we had very beautiful *ongei Shabbat*, and we would put on very beautiful skits. We had Israeli dancing and sang Israeli songs, and we had a variety of other cultural activities.

We had two *madrichot* (women counselors) with us from Lodz. Dorka did not come with us, but Lopek, a new man, replaced her in the kibbutz. Lopek was like an army drill sergeant. He made us run, jump, pull all kinds of ropes, do push-ups, regular exercise, anything and everything. Every once in a while, he would also teach us some Hebrew songs. And many times, he liked to show off. I remember once, he taught us a song, and he did not explain the Hebrew meaning well; I believe it was my sister Bracha (Beatrice) who asked him the meaning of a word, and of course he didn't know and was very embarrassed. I don't think anyone ever asked him to explain anything again.

As time went on, we got to know the camp much better; it was a military base. We found out that beneath the camp, there were tremendous tunnels that were running kilometers and kilometers, and that there were all kinds of weapons in those tunnels. We found bayonets, bullets, mines, all kinds of things, and we did not dare to go very deep into these tunnels. Only just a few hundred meters, perhaps not even that far, and we came up with all these weapons. We also found a variety of weapons such as bullets, mines, and pistols in the wooded area surrounding the camp. Additionally, we had bombed-out airplanes all around us, and when we explored the cockpits, we found guns. There were little bottles containing acid all over the area. As a matter of fact, I was told that before we came to the camp, a friend of mine, a boy by the name of Khune, who was not in the kibbutz but who lived in the same block as my parents, took a little bottle and threw it at another boy. The bottle broke open, and the acid burned the young man's entire face. At a later time, that boy was sent on *aliyah bet* (illegal immigration) to Israel. All the weapons that we had found, we turned over to the adults. We later learned that the important weapons somehow found their way to Palestine.

Khune was a young man who became greatly disturbed after he lost his father. He only had his mother, and I remember her very well. She was a very nice, highly intelligent woman, and after a short while, she remarried a wonderful man who had lost his entire family. This same Khune one day collected a number of bullets, made a little fire, put the bullets into the fire, and positioned himself in back of a tree, watching to see what would happen. Suddenly the bullets began shooting all over the place. People did not know what was going on. One young boy was hit in the shoulder by a bullet, and during all this pandemonium, Khune was lying down, watching and enjoying every moment. Sadly, the camp had no facilities or professionals to help him. Another time he caught a number of cats and strung them up on a rope across the pool. His mother was beside herself, but there was nothing she could do. Within a year she died, and Khune remained only with his stepfather, who treated him as if he were his own son.

In Leipheim, ours was the only children's kibbutz, but in camp, we had many other kibbutzim. Barrack #8, right next to us, was the Shomer Ha'tza'ir kibbutz (pro-Communist–anti-religious). These were people in their twenties and early thirties. Not far from us as well, Barrack #16 was the adult kibbutz Dror. This was the kibbutz from Lodz that watched over us. Barracks #17 and #18 were the kibbutz Yichud, also adults. Barracks #22, #24, and #26 were partisans. These were people who survived the war in the forests. In the center of the camp, there were a number of barracks that were "independent." They did not belong to any party at all. In addition to the school, we had a theater, a number of synagogues, a ritual bath, a public kitchen, a sports club, and a very good soccer team. It is easy to see that in our camp, with all these parties and organizations, we emulated what was happening in Palestine (Israel). It was a miniature state. In camp we had to attend a regular Hebrew school from nine o'clock in the morning until two o'clock in the afternoon. Now I realize that the school curriculum was based upon the curriculum of the schools in Palestine. Every subject was taught in Hebrew. Every once in a while we had teachers from

Israel teach us. Among the subjects taught were Hebrew, English, math, physics, grammar, geography, Jewish History, and Bible. Students were literally forced to speak the language, and after a short time, a year and a half or so, most of us learned to speak Hebrew quite well. Many of the teachers were very devoted people, and they tried very much to help us. One of the teachers that comes to mind is a man by the name of Mariosh. He taught us not only Hebrew and history, but many times he tried to teach us etiquette. He taught us how to eat properly, how not to eat with an open mouth, and how to tip our hats in respect when we walked in the street and saw somebody older or a lady. He taught us not to speak with our hands, to cover our mouths when we coughed, and all kinds of other tips. These were little things but important things, because very few kids had the proper upbringing. This terrible war did not permit us to behave or learn the proper behavior. Some grew up in forests, some grew up in camps, and some grew up in concentration camps—all kinds of places. We never worried about how to eat; during the war we always worried about what to eat. As long as you got ahold of something to eat, that was the important thing. But unfortunately, very few paid attention to what Mariosh tried to do. As we grew older, we realized more and more what this man tried to do for us. I remember the day after he taught us about tipping our hats for an older person, my friend Yisroel Litmanovitch and I were walking around in camp, and along came Mariosh with his girlfriend; we walked past him and tipped our hats to show him what we learned in his class, and then we walked around them again so that we could tip our hats to them yet again. We did this at least three or four times, if not more. The following day, when we came to school, Mariosh took time out to explain to us that when we saw someone and tipped our hats, once was sufficient. There was absolutely no need to walk around them a second or third time to tip your hat again. He didn't mention any names, but we knew exactly who he meant; we got the message.

My sister, Bracha, was probably the top student in our school. Whenever we had a visiting dignitary, whether he was from America or from Palestine/Israel, my sister would be the one to greet him. Whether it was the school or the kibbutz, she was the one to represent us. She spoke a very beautiful Hebrew, and she was honored with this task. I think the highest dignitary that ever came to our camp was Yitzchak Greenbaum, who was a representative of the Jews in the Polish senate before the war, and later a Knesset member. Thousands of people came out to see him, and my sister welcomed him. I never had the honor of greeting anyone. I was not one of the outstanding students. I was a pretty decent student who tried to have as much fun as possible and not worry about too many other things. We tried to catch up on all the fun we missed during the war, when we forgot how to be children. In our school, we had a cafeteria. No hot foods were served—only a sandwich of bread, cheese and butter.

For every Chanukah and Purim (Fast of Esther) we put on a play in Hebrew. That was when we had the greatest of times. On Chanukah, we would put on the play *Chanah and Her Seven Sons*, or Sholom Aleichem's play called *Chanukah Gelt*. On Purim, we also put on a Sholom Aleichem play. I used to participate in these plays. Hundreds of people from the camp would come and watch our performances. They were magnificent. I think the people enjoyed our plays more than the professional theater that we had in camp.

Part of the school's program was also going on field trips. The field trips were not just for a day or a few hours, but they involved going for a number of days and sometimes close to a week. I remember one trip we went on was next to Badreichenhall. There were beautiful lakes between the mountains, and it was not far from Berchtesgarten. We saw Hitler's home, the Eagle's Nest (Adlerhof), high above on a mountaintop. We went by boat on these magnificent lakes between the mountains, and when somebody would sound the horn on the boat, you could hear the echo in the mountains. We visited palaces of German kings and Bavarian kings. They were the most magnificent things we saw. One palace we entered had a huge Star of David on a wall, and we got very excited. We all wondered what a Star of David was doing in a German king's palace. So I remember they called over one of the German guides and asked him to explain this phenomenon. He looked at it and said that this was only a geometric figure. He knew nothing of the Jewish symbol, or maybe he didn't want to know anything about it. So he explained to us that it was a geometric figure, and that was why it was on the wall. Another time, I remember, we went to a salt mine where we descended about a mile deep beneath the ground. They had a little salt lake there. We put on special rubber garments, so as not to get wet, and there were little boats that took us around in that little salt lake. We traveled to many different parts of Germany with the school. Sometimes, we would use those huge American Studebaker trucks if the groups were small and the distance wasn't too great. And when more than one class participated, we traveled by train. When we did use trucks, we would put a Jewish flag on that truck, and we would sing songs as we drove through Germany. If we had dared to do this in Poland, all of us would have been killed.

One of the nicest trips that I can recall taking was a trip for boys only that lasted for about four weeks. This trip was to Closta Etal, probably one of the most beautiful areas that I have seen in my life. There was a monastery in Etal, and we stayed in this monastery. They gave us one wing of six or seven rooms. The area was just magnificent; it was all mountains and forests. Each mountain was more beautiful than the other. The mountains were so high that many times when it was cloudy, we could see the clouds get stuck on the mountains, and sometimes, when the clouds would be a little lower, we could see the peaks sticking out from above the clouds. It looked like a wonderland. And when it rained there, it would start suddenly and come down in buckets; just as suddenly, it would stop completely. The amount of rain that came down was unbelievable.

We climbed these mountains, especially the lower ones, and in one place I remember, we came to the top of a mountain and noticed a small area where water was seeping through. We cleared away the area, and suddenly it was a little water spring. We drank this water, and it was delicious, and many times we would come just to that spot to drink the water.

Etal was located just a few kilometers outside of Garmisch Partenkirchen, where they had the Zugspitze, which is probably the tallest mountain in Germany, 9,721 feet above sea level, and among the tallest mountains in Europe. At the Zugspitze, we went up with a special cable car, and when we came there we noticed a wall with Yiddish written on it: "*Amcha kakt oif der veld und fort veiter*," which loosely translated means, "The Jewish people crap on the world and keep on traveling." What was really meant by this was that we survived, we will go on, and no one will stop us. We looked at it, and we were pleased, because to us it was a sign of courage.

In Etal, no matter how much food they gave us, it was not sufficient. But then again, they did not give us that much food, because we were always hungry. So we looked around and we tried to help ourselves. We went around in that town, and we found a little factory where they were making lemonade. We somehow took a liking to this lemonade, and everybody in the group would go into that little factory, buy a couple of bottles of lemonade, and keep it under the beds. And every once in a while, when we felt a little bit hungry, we would drink this lemonade.

There were also German children in this monastery, but they were in the opposite wing from us. We had no contact with them. They were not permitted to come close to us, and we were not permitted to come close to them, because they feared confrontations, and rightfully so. We played soccer on separate fields from each other. We complained of not having enough food, and they used to gather in their areas and chant constantly, *"We haben hunger, we haben hunger"* ("We are hungry, we are hungry"). But we did not have contact.

There were two dining rooms. The German group had the first dining room, which was the larger of the two because they had a larger group, and we had the second dining room. In order to get into our room, we had to pass through theirs. That was the only time we saw their faces. In their dining room, there was a crucifix. In ours, there were no religious symbols. I remember that one of the heads of the monastery came over to one of our group leaders and requested that when we enter the dining room, we should remove our hats. Our group leader did not reject the request. He came to us and told us about it. As soon as we heard this request, we were very angry. Subsequently, even the boys who did not wear hats at all put on a hat. Everyone wore a hat. No matter what the group leader said to us, we insisted on keeping the hats on. The anger was so strong that the least thing that we could do to hurt their feelings, we were happy to do.

The food there was not only insufficient, it was awful. The piece of bread they gave us was so thin it was transparent. The soup was atrocious, and once, when they served us the soup, there were little worms in it. One boy, a friend of mine from the kibbutz, looked in the soup, and when he saw these little worms, it upset him no end. He got up and made his way to a little dais where the physician, a German Jew who accompanied us from our camp, was sitting. He went over to him and very politely said to him in

Yiddish, "Please take a look, there are worms in the soup." The doctor looked at the soup, and he answered him in German, "Yes, this is very healthy." By that time, the boy lost his patience, looked at the doctor, and said, *"Fres dach oon alein mit dem. Du kenst meins auchet uben,"* which, loosely translated, means "Go stuff yourself with the soup, and you can have mine too." He left the soup on his table and walked away.

After about two weeks, we were really hungry. We did not want to chant as the German kids were doing. We decided to take some action instead. A few older boys were sent back to the DP Camp to explain the situation in the hope of improving it. Within a day or two, they came back with more food and more bread . . . especially bread. That was a little bit better.

In this monastery, we were asked to behave in a certain way. The monks looked at us, watched us, but we did not permit them to interfere in our daily activities. We had to be in bed at nine o'clock, and one evening before we went to sleep a bat got into the room. We were about ten or twelve kids in our room, and we wanted very much to catch that bat. We had heard that bats' wings have beautiful colors, and we wanted to see that. So we designated one of the boys as guard next to the door. He needed to listen for anyone coming and signal us if someone was approaching our door. Then we went to work on catching the bat. Each of us in the room armed himself with his pillow, and as the bat flew around in the room we tried to knock him down. Every time we would make noise a monk would start out toward our room, our guard would give the signal, the lights would be turned off, and each of us would be on his bed. When the monk opened the door, it was quiet. He closed the door, went away, and we started all over again. This went on for a little while. Finally, finally, we managed to knock the bat down. We held it down, opened the wings, and the thing looked more like a big mouse than a bird. The colors of the wings were nice. We put it away, wrapped someplace, but when we got up in the morning, the bat was not there.

All in all, it was a magnificent place. Even though we were hungry, the beauty of the place made up for it. I do remember the shock that I had when I walked around Etal and I noticed my family name Bichler all over the place, even on some monuments, and it was unbelievable. I did not realize it was a German or Austrian name. Obviously, it was very popular there, and these people were not our relatives. These were Germans. Etal was a beautiful place. I still remember it quite well. And it was probably the place where I had one of the greatest times in my youth. The school, the field trips, and our freedom of movement made us feel again like normal human beings. We enjoyed every moment of it.

A number of months after we came to camp, my parents decided that the regular Hebrew school was not sufficient for me. They said, "A school is a school and religious instructions are religious instructions." Since we left Turkistan, I had not received any religious instructions. Therefore my mother went to Esther, the *madricha*, and told her she wanted me to attend Talmud Torah, a Jewish religious school that is attended in the afternoons following secular school, and that I should be excused from all the other activities of the kibbutz. Now mind you, our kibbutz was not religious, nor was it pro-religion. My parents did not send me to the kibbutz because of the political ideologies, but rather because it enabled us to be smuggled out of Poland. Since we were out of Poland, Jewish education was the top priority. My mother came to Esther and told her this. Esther was not opposed, because she probably realized that if she did not give in to my parents' wishes they would remove me from the kibbutz. She probably also realized that if one student left the kibbutz because of religious instruction, many others would do the same. Perhaps she herself sympathized with my mother, because she too had a mother with

her in the kibbutz, and I was able to see that her mother conducted herself in the same manner as my mother and my grandmother, lighting candles, watching what she ate, and Esther herself
knew quite a bit about religion.

I was registered to attend Talmud Torah. The principal of the
Talmud Torah was a Polish Jew, Rabbi Eliezer Kagel, a lovely gentleman with a nice long white beard and *payos* (side curls). The
instructor in the Talmud Torah was a Hungarian rabbi. He was a
very strict individual and not too clean, unfortunately. He wore a
black hat. It was thick and heavy. I was positive that one could
squeeze oil out of this hat. We always looked at this individual and
made fun of him. He taught us not only to pray but also how to put
on tefillin. We were at that time thirteen years old. There was no
such thing as having bar mitzvahs when we were on the move. So
I knew that I was thirteen, and I was told to put on tefillin. Once
in a while I would use my father's tefillin. The Hungarian rabbi was
teaching us how to put on tefillin that we received from a Jewish
organization. Two of my other friends from the kibbutz, Chaim
Tzierel's and Mendel Kochol, were together with me. And here we
were, one day, putting on tefillin, and I don't know how, but
Mendel got ahold of a piece of gum and was chewing it. I should
note here that it is forbidden to eat while putting on tefillin. The
rabbi did not know that it was a piece of gum—nobody in Europe
went around chewing gum—so he probably thought that Mendel
was eating while he was putting on his tefillin. In the middle of the
room, there was an iron stove. Near the stove, there were pieces of
wood. The rabbi picked up a piece of wood and smacked Mendel
on his arm because he was eating while he was putting on tefillin.
His arm swelled up, and he was in a lot of pain. Finally, when we
came home from *cheder* (Talmud Torah), Mendel's father noticed
his arm was swollen. He asked what happened, and Mendel told
him that the rabbi smacked him with a piece of wood. His father

asked why, and he told him that he was chewing a piece of gum, at which point his father said, "While you were putting on tefillin you were chewing?" And with that, he took off his belt and hit Mendel with it. It was so bad that for a day or so he couldn't move. I don't think he ever chewed again when he put on tefillin. This is just one example of the behavior of this rabbi in the Talmud Torah.

I was with this Hungarian rabbi for a short period of time since I was more advanced because of the religious instruction I had received in Turkistan. Therefore, I started studying with the principal, Rabbi Kagal, along with a few other students, and we began to study a little Talmud. The Talmud Torah was quite nice. We had a little fun, especially when we studied with Rabbi Kagal. He was always busy; he was a little bit of a politician, and we used to get treats. Sometimes we would get apples, and once a week or once every two weeks, we would get a piece of chocolate. It was American chocolate, and the box was covered with a wax in order to preserve it. Every once in a while we would get a piece of this chocolate. When we got the chocolate, if it was a sealed bar, I never dared to open it. Even when I was in the kibbutz, I would bring it to my parents, who also seldom broke it open, not even for my little sister Iris (Chaya). They used to take these sealed chocolates and either sell them or exchange them for other food. Very seldom, when Rabbi Kagal did not have enough sealed chocolates for everyone, he would break the boxes open and split the chocolate into pieces. Then, and only then, would I eat a piece of it and bring the rest home. But when the piece was really small, I would eat it without bringing any home. I should emphasize—I was never told by my parents to bring it home. I did this on my own because I knew that we could use the money from it for other things. It was sort of a responsibility for the family. None of us would ever take anything for ourselves. Whether it was my sister, my mother, my father, or I, we always thought of the entire family first.

I was one of the youngest who studied with Rabbi Kagel. The others were about two or three years older, some even more than that. One of the boys who studied with Rabbi Kagel but in a different group was, and still is, my good friend Morris Katz, the very famous fastest painter in the world (*Guinness World Records* 1980). I remember how he always walked about with a sketchbook in hand, always sketching landscapes. Morris survived the war with his mother and brother. In 1943, he was liberated by the Russian army from a slave labor camp in Tluster, about fifteen miles from the Rumanian border. That moment of liberation is engraved in his mind forever. He remembers the very heavy gunfire followed by one Russian soldier appearing on a horse. The Jews in the camp kissed the horse's feet. They thought its rider was the Messiah. Then, five Russian tanks arrived and started shouting to the people to take cover—that German planes were coming—and with that two German planes suddenly materialized and began bombing and strafing the barracks. Morris ran and somehow dodged the bullets. Two of the soldiers shot down one of the planes, and the second plane flew off. The Soviets apprehended the German leaders of the slave labor camp, then assembled the Jews and asked them what to do with the Germans. One Jew asked permission to bite off the nose of the camp's commander; permission was granted. Such were the sufferings of the Jews during the war that they were brought to these subhuman levels. The Jew went up on the platform where the Germans were being held and bit off the commander's nose. The Russians then did away with the Germans. It was 1946 when Morris with his mother and brother finally reached a DP Camp in the American zone in Germany. That was when we met and became friends.

Every so often, Rabbi Kagel decided to have some fun with us and would say, "Okay, let's see who can eat the most . . . ," and a contest would ensue. At that time in our lives we were no longer

walking around hungry. We all had good appetites and made wor-
thy contestants. All in all, we had quite a bit of fun. I remember one
afternoon, we were sitting and studying, and an American truck
pulled up in front of the synagogue where the Talmud Torah was,
and in it was a load of holy books. These books had been buried at
a cemetery for the duration of the war. They began to unload these
books, and I noticed one that made an impression on me. I showed
it to Rabbi Kagel, and I asked him if it was okay for me to take this
book. He looked at it and he said, "Yes, you can have it." The book
was the entire twenty-four books of the Bible written in Yiddish. It
was printed in Amsterdam in 1667 and included a blessing for the
authorities written in Latin. I still have the book today. Being in the
principal's class can certainly have its perks.

Twenty-One

As I had said, Leipheim was situated amid beautiful surroundings. And my friends and I decided not only to enjoy the beauty, but also to partake of what was growing in the orchards and fields. So what we kids did when we knew that the fruits were ripe was organize ourselves into groups, raid the orchards, and pick the fruits. But there were times when we were very careless, perhaps on purpose. We not only took the fruits but also broke off the branches from the trees. We just didn't care. About one hundred feet away from our camp's soccer field was a poppy field. We used to go into the field and break open the poppies and eat them to our delight. Fortunately, we had no idea about the narcotic effects of their flowers and left them alone. A Jewish policeman stood guard right outside the camp's gates where there was a field with a nice patch of gooseberries and currents. When we wanted to get to that field, we would first walk past the field, make a U-turn, and crawl on our bellies into the patch so the policeman wouldn't see us. We would eat as much as we wanted, and then we would put as much as we wanted into our shirts and make our getaway. We only had to watch out for the Jewish police; we did not fear the Germans. We feared our own police because they did not permit us to do these things. All of this harvesting was okay for about a year or two, because a little later the Germans began feeling that they were the owners again, and we had to be very, very careful. Some orchards were fenced around; the Germans sometimes let dogs loose on us, so we had to be extremely careful, and we soon stopped raiding those orchards because we were afraid of the dogs. We only raided where we felt safe.

We had very little to do with the Germans. Only once in a while, we would take a little sugar to a place where they would make a particular candy for us that we liked. I would also go there once in a while for a haircut. Eventually, we were told that the water was not good in Bavaria, and my parents would give me empty bottles to take into Leipheim where we would buy beer. The beer wasn't really beer; it was more like water, and this is what we drank. And once I had a bicycle, my mother used to prepare whatever she wanted to bake, and I would ride them over to the baker in Leipheim where he would bake them for us. This was the interaction between the Germans and us. The adults had a little bit more contact with the Germans since they bartered with them. But as far as sports or schooling went, we had no contact with the Germans except for music lessons that some of us took.

Life in the kibbutz continued as I described until about June or July 1947, when the *madrichim* began making preparations for part of our group to go on *aliyah bet*, which was an illegal immigration to Palestine. The youth that were chosen for *aliyah bet* were orphaned or with only one parent. They totaled about thirty children. It was a clandestine operation, and we knew nothing of these plans. One morning we got up and half of our kibbutz was gone, along with most of the *madrichim*. They were transported with many other people to France or Italy where they boarded a ship to Palestine. It was the famous Exodus of August 1947. The ship made it to Haifa, Palestine. After a bitter fight with the British, they were forcibly returned with their ship to Europe. The passengers languished in agony in a port in France and refused to leave the ship. Sometime later the ship's refugee passengers were returned to Hamburg, Germany, but our kibbutz members never returned to our camp.

After the members of our kibbutz left, nothing was the same. Not too long after that an argument broke out between me and Chayim, a young man from the kibbutz who was older than me and who thought of himself as a leader. The argument was because he practiced favoritism, and I didn't care very much for that. So following the argument, I went into my room, took a few rags, wrapped them in my blanket, and walked out of the kibbutz and went to my parents. A few days after I left, my sister, my cousin, and most of the other children who had parents left the kibbutz and moved in with their parents. The kibbutz, for all practical purposes, disbanded. And once the kibbutz no longer existed, most of the parents who lived in Block #6 or adjacent blocks in small rooms were given permission to move with their kids to Barrack #9, one family in one room, where the kibbutz used to be housed. The rooms in Barrack #9 were much larger. We moved to the second floor, and most of my friends did the same thing. Practically the entire barrack was in the hands of the parents and the children who at one time belonged to the kibbutz. My uncle lived three doors away from us. At this point in time he was already married to Aunt Rivka for about two years. They had a little boy by the name of Yitzchak. My aunt and uncle with their new son, my uncle's daughter, Chaya, and my grandmother were all in one room. Finally, the family was together. My father and uncle worked in the public kitchen. A little after the disbandment of the kibbutz an afternoon Yeshiva was opened in camp under the auspices of American Jews (one of them was Dean Zar of Yeshiva University). The Rosh

Yeshiva, the Head of the Yeshiva, was Rabbi Yankale Gallinski. I remember him quite well. He was about five feet tall. He had a beautiful wife and a few children. When the Yeshiva opened, most of the boys from the Talmud Torah ended up in this Yeshiva. Here we studied the Five Books of Moses with the Rashi commentary, as well as Talmud. Joseph, Rabbi Gallinski's assistant, taught us a little bit of how to lead the services, and every so often, one of us would go up and try to lead. Joseph was a bachelor and a very dedicated man. He and the rabbi were both wonderful human beings.

Our great love was sports, and in the cold winter months when the days were short, we wanted to play soccer after school. We convinced the Rosh Yeshiva to persuade our teacher to permit us to come to learn as early as 5:30 in the morning. We would all come with candles; we would sit, we would learn, and then we would pray and then hurry home to eat breakfast and go to school, and once school was over, we would be able to play soccer. He accommodated us, and we appreciated it very much. I believe because of what he did for us, we paid more attention, and we probably learned more in the mornings than we did in the afternoons when we were thinking of soccer. He knew psychology quite well, and we all benefited very much. This Yeshiva in our camp lasted for about a year, and then they tried to encourage the students in this Yeshiva to transfer to an all-day Yeshiva in Salzburg. To my knowledge very few people actually went to Salzburg. The only one I can remember that did go was my friend Zalman. The rest of us went back to study with Rabbi Eliezer Kagel. This Zalman was the son of a shoemaker whose name was Feivel Pfeffer. Zalman shaved his head, leaving only his two *payos*, and went to Salzburg. He was in Salzburg for a number of months and then came home for Passover. When he was home for Passover, he took a few of his mother's pots on his bicycle and rode to Leipheim to a blacksmith to burn them out well to make sure that they would be purely kosher for Passover. His father did not interfere, but I do remember him telling me, "You will see. This is not going to last for very long, because that's exactly what my brother did and then he became a nonbeliever." Unfortunately, the prophecy of his father came true. During my first trip to Israel, in 1956, my uncle saw Feivel and told him that I was visiting. Zalman, who was a lieutenant in heavy artillery in the Israeli army, came to see me, but he came on a Shabbat, riding a motorcycle. I was in shock because I remembered him as an orthodox boy. He came in, very friendly, very nice, and he told me that Yankale Gallinski, our Rosh Yeshiva, was living in the neighboring town of B'nei Brak, an ultraorthodox area near my uncle. Zalman said that whenever he could, he made a point of riding past the Rosh Yeshiva's house on his motorcycle on Shabbat just to remind him that his father's prophecy came true.

I continued studying with Rabbi Kagel until the camp closed down at the beginning of 1949, but the studying was different. A number of kids dropped out. The groups were smaller, and after we finished studying, we did not rush home. We remained in the synagogue to pray with the adults. We began mingling with the adults, and we participated in the evening services. And a number of times, I would remain to listen to the stories between the afternoon and evening prayers. I especially enjoyed listening to the stories of one man. His name was Mr. Antman, may he rest in peace. His sons were my friends, and he had 1001 stories, always dealing with devils. Stories of how he himself saw the devils. There was one story he told where as he took out a cigarette, a devil came out and wanted to give him a light, and to take fire from a devil meant death . . . . These stories used to frighten me sometimes, and I'd be afraid to walk home, especially if I had to cross an intersection; because according to another of Mr. Antman's stories, if you have two roads that form a cross, at the place they cross, you definitely have devils. And every time I came close to an intersection it would frighten the daylights out of me, because I thought devils would come out. After a while, I got myself a flashlight, and it helped me to walk home in the dark. This went on for about half a year until the camp was liquidated.

I loved to play soccer; the soccer field was right outside our door. There was a bench near a little fence. We jumped on that bench, over the fence, and we were on the soccer field. We played soccer whenever we had a free moment, whether it was the summer or winter. In the summer, we would get up early in the morning and immediately go out on the field. Many times, my grandma would bring me some food to the field, and if she had not brought out the food, I would probably have forgotten to eat. By the end of 1947 or beginning of 1948, a beautiful swimming pool was built near the soccer field. It was magnificent! We would swim, and then we would play soccer. We would play soccer, then we would swim. We played soccer in the summer barefoot because we couldn't afford shoes. We also played soccer of course in the winter in the snow. Soccer was almost like a religion to us.

Because I was so skinny, my father did not want me to run around too much. He thought that I was so skinny as a result of playing soccer. Therefore I had to be careful and keep a watch out for my father. Everyone knew that if anyone saw my father coming, I would have to be told immediately so that I could hide. If it was a cool day, I would lie down, and they would cover me with the coats until my father went by. And when it was warm enough, I would just stand by the goalie and watch, as if I were very passive and was not playing, until Father went by. As soon as he left, I'd be right back in the game as usual.

We loved playing soccer, but that required a soccer ball. So at the beginning, when we couldn't get our hands on a soccer ball, we would improvise and make balls out of rags. Sometimes we even kicked cans around. We did anything in order to play soccer; just to kick and run was a great thing. We had one boy in camp that lived in the partisan blocks, and he always spoke Polish (his name was Michael). He had very close relatives in America, and they sent him everything. He was the only kid who received roller skates in camp. We didn't even know what they were, but he was scooting around on these roller skates. He was excellent on them. He also got a soccer ball from them, and because of this soccer ball, he was very popular. So he would come with that soccer ball, and he would have the privilege of picking the teams. And we had to make sure that his team would be winning at certain times, because if he didn't like what was happening on the field, he would pick up the ball and just walk off the field. We had to use psychology to make sure that we could play soccer.

I was quite good at this sport. Many times I played center, center forward. Our trainer was a Hungarian Jew. His name was Yoshka and he was a professional; he played for the #1 Hungarian team before the war. He trained the team in our camp, and he trained us too. At times we had exhibition games; we played other youth. Sometimes we even played against Team #2 in our camp just for practice purposes, and we would give them a run for their money. However, I was never able to play in any of these official games because my father wouldn't permit me. I was quite good at kicking goals in, and I tried to convince him to let me play, but to no avail. I saw that it bothered him very much; he knew how much I loved the game, but he would not give me permission to play because he worried it would be detrimental to my health, and as a result, I never participated in any official games. I watched, my heart would go out to my friends, my friends looked at me, but I just was not permitted to get on the field.

Now, one of the most moving things that happened to me and to the other young boys was when we played soccer on the field.

One of us fell in a place, and he realized it was a very soft spot. We knew from experience that if there is a soft spot in a field, there's a good possibility that something is buried beneath. So, we went over to the place, and we began digging slowly. And to our great amazement and shock, we came up with a rag, and in the rag were a number of pieces of soap. This soap was made from the fats of Jewish people. On the soap was written "Rheines Yiddishe Zeifhe, Pure Jewish Soap." We stood there, unable to move and not knowing what to do. We all knew what it meant. We left it, we stood up, we looked at it, we looked at each other, and then we ran to call our parents. And when the parents came, they took the rags with these few pieces of soap—maybe three or four pieces of soap—and brought them to the rabbi of the camp. The leaders of the camp arranged for a mass funeral, and everybody in the camp, young and old, participated in the funeral and burial of these few pieces of soap. The funeral took place in a nearby German town, Ginsburg, which had a large Jewish cemetery. Apparently some time ago, many Jews must have lived in the Ginsburg area.

Perhaps I should mention the infamous Mengele,* the angel of death, was born and lived in Ginsburg. Perhaps its worthwhile mentioning that while we lived in the camp, his entire family, and perhaps he too, lived there. Even after he ran away, his family remained living there; here we had thousands of Jews living five kilometers away, yet no one did anything to his family. At times, I think about it and cannot understand how we could let them live in peace when practically everyone in camp lost most of their families. The Jews after the war never spoke of revenge. I never heard

---

* Josef Mengele was appointed doctor in Auschwitz at his own request. From 1943–1945 he initiated a series of cruel experiments which caused the death of many Jewish inmates. Mengele was interested in research on twins, which frequently involved killing both at the same time to compare the organs. He injected children in the eyes to change their eye color. He ordered gypsies killed in order to possess their eyes. He participated in the selection of tens of thousands of prisoners destined to die in the gas chambers.

anyone say let's go and kill Germans, or let's go and burn the home of Mengele's family. Go figure out the Jewish people—it's very difficult. We are a complex people, and it is difficult to anticipate our behavior, even after such a terrible Holocaust. I never heard Mengele's name mentioned in camp or in school. No one spoke of his or her sufferings. We suffered in silence and cried with tears of blood. Many people lived and at the same time did not live. They wanted to be here, and they wanted to be with the families they lost. They were swaying between this world and the world to come. Many felt guilty for surviving the war.

The only other time in our camp where great masses of people participated in a funeral, as a matter of fact at the same cemetery, was when our principal, Mr. Shulman, may he rest in peace, was brought to his eternal rest. Mr. Shulman, who was so devoted and who built such a beautiful and wonderful school for us, did not have any family. They were all slaughtered. He was the only one of his family who survived.

At about this time Father discovered that some of his cousins from the Brenners of Zamosc survived and were living in the DP Camp in Deggendorff, Germany. He went immediately to see them. They were his Uncle Chaim's two daughters, Mania and Hadassa—Mania with her son, Izzy, and Hadassa and their nephew, Benny. From Mania and Hadassa, Father learned that Uncle Chaim and his wife, Chava, along with their four children, two of whom had their own families, all left Zamosc at the same time as the Russian army was withdrawing from the city. This family of eleven people wandered around for months and finally ended up in Pinsk. In the summer of 1940 the USSR offered all Polish nationals Soviet citizenship. The Brenner family rejected the Soviet offer. Soon thereafter, in the middle of the night, police came to their apartment, gave them forty-five minutes to collect their belongings, and drove them to the railroad depot. At the station were thousands of others. All the people were packed into cattle cars, and after a four-week journey, they arrived into Archangel, Siberia. From there they were sent to a labor camp in the Taiga forest. The men logged wood from dawn to dusk and received four hundred grams of bread per day. Women and children were given less.

Fourteen months later the Soviet Union, in a pact with the exiled government of Poland in London, granted amnesty "to all Polish citizens now detained in the Soviet territory." The Brenners were free to leave the slave labor camp. After a four-week journey they arrived in Gizhduva. They moved to a kolkhoz, a collective farm, near the city of Dzambul, Kazakhstan. Soon after settling in the kolkhoz, Rachel took ill. She was taken to the hospital and within a day, she died at the age of forty-two. Four months later, Saul Katz (Cousin Mania's husband) developed internal bleeding and bled for two days. Finally, after much trying, an ox and buggy were provided to take him to the hospital. He died in the wagon. He was thirty-nine. At that time, Uncle Chaim was ailing and was not told of Saul's passing. Ten days later Uncle Chaim died, and six months following his death, Aunt Chava died.

Early in 1943 all men were rounded up for the *trudovoy front* to work behind the front lines. Rueven and Joshua were sent off at the same time and never returned. They were each sent to a different camp, but both died of overwork, undernourishment, and disease. Out of a family of eleven people, only two adults, Mania and Hadassa, and two children, Mania's son Izzy and Mania's and Hadassa's nephew Benny, survived. Mania and Hadassa cared for and loved Benny as only mothers could.

In 1945 the remainder of the family moved out of the kolkhoz to the city of Dzambul in search of a better livelihood. Finally, in 1946 Mania was able to obtain transportation by freight train back to Poland. Weeks later their train arrived to Stetin. From Stetin,

Mania alone went back to her hometown of Zamosc, where a lawyer, her brother Joshua's colleague, helped her sell the family property for very little. When Mania returned to Stetin she used that money to buy four places on a jeep to travel underground to the American sector of Berlin to the DP Camp in Templehoff, where they remained for approximately two years. At the time of the Russian blockade of Berlin, they left Temlehoff by a U.S. transport plane that had brought supplies to Berlin and settled in Deggendorff DP Camp.

Twenty-Two

Life was not bad in camp. For the kids it was excellent. We played soccer, we ate, and we went to school. We had nothing to worry about. There was nothing there, and there was nothing we could do. Everything was temporary.

We lived in the camp, we got our rations, and every once in a while we would get a pair of shoes and a pair of pants. We, the kids, tried to make up as much as possible for what we missed during the war, and we enjoyed ourselves very much.

I was extremely skinny, and in the summer of 1948, a doctor recommended that I and a few other kids in camp should be sent off to a sanitarium to gain weight. My parents agreed, and the few kids who went there had to turn in their ration cards and were taken to a sanitarium that was outside of Stuttgart. The sanitarium itself was a very beautiful building with lovely grounds all fenced in. At the gate, a Jewish policeman stood guard, and we had to identify ourselves in order to be permitted to enter. The kids were not permitted to go outside unless a counselor took us out. They fed us three times a day. The food was not anything special. Too much food was not given. There were no sweets, ice cream, chocolate, or cake that would help you put on weight. The only way they wanted us to put on weight was through restricting our movement by making us rest and rest and rest. They would read stories to us; they would try to put on plays with us. And many times we were quite hungry, and we were wondering whether they were doing what they were supposed to do for us. I'm positive that they received plenty of goodies for us from the authorities, but somehow, we didn't get any of them. If that weren't enough, we heard stories from some counselors that the building we were in served as a place where they killed Jewish children by throwing them off the roofs, head first, during the war. I don't know whether or not this was true, but when we heard these stories, we also lost our appetites. Truthfully speaking, we felt more as though we were in a jail than in a sanitarium, especially with the fence and guard around us. We did put on a few skits, but when we complained about the food, they just encouraged us to rest and nothing else.

I was extremely miserable, and I wrote a few cards home, telling my parents about it. I was very depressed because somehow I felt that my freedom was taken away by having to walk around in a fenced-in yard guarded by police. So after a number of weeks, my parents sent my sister Bracha to visit me. My sister came in, she saw what was going on, and when I explained the situation to her and told her that I had no intention of remaining there, we made a plan. She was to carry out my few belongings in her bag, and I had already found a place where I could climb over the fence without being noticed and take off. This plan was put into action. We carefully put my belongings into my sister's bag. I had noticed that she crossed the gate without any problem, and I went to the spot where it was possible to climb over that fence, and I escaped. We went to the railroad station, bought tickets, and came home to Leipheim.

I was delighted to be back in camp with my friends. But there was one problem, and that was how to get back my ration card.

Without it, my parents could not get any food, clothing, or shoes for me. So my father and I went to the director of the camp, a Canadian lady, and I explained to her what happened. She did not want to believe me, since it had taken a great deal of effort on her part to get me into the sanitarium. It was supposed to be very healthy. She worried for us. But I told her that instead of gaining weight, I lost weight, and instead of feeding us, they gave us less food and more rest, and we were virtually in a modern prison. She was unhappy, but in the end she had no choice, and my ration card was given back to my father.

The director of the camp was a very interesting person. We were positive that she knew what was going on, because many illegal transports to Palestine originated in our camp, and I am sure that she not only knew about it but also probably helped out with it. They used to bring food and people into our camps during the night. Huge American Studebaker trucks would line up in our camp, these trucks would be loaded with the food and the people in the middle of the night, and they'd be sent off either to Italy or to France, where they would be taken to ships on their way to Palestine. She had to have known about it.

When I came back from the sanitarium, my parents took one look at me and approved of what I had done. I was sent to the sanitarium to gain weight and instead, I was miserable and lost weight. Life in camp, as far as we were concerned, was good; it was wonderful, as a matter of fact. The camp was an entity of its own. We had a theater that doubled as a movie house. They used to bring Yiddish films from the United States. We saw *Yiedl mit dem Fiedl*, *The Dibbuk*, *Tkiat Kav*, *Green Fields*, and many, many others. We also had a very, very good soccer team. The Jewish DP Camps in Germany had a soccer league, and its teams played each other.

Leipheim was probably one of the finest teams in Germany. Eight players of our first team were Hungarians, and three were

Polish Jews. Our main competitor was Landsberg. It was a much bigger camp. Most of their players were Polish Jews. Landsberg was at least twice the size of Leipheim, but our team was better. Many of the matches took place on a Saturday, and practically everyone in camp except for the ultraorthodox would come out to see the match. The rabbi and the people around him, of course, did not like the idea, and they would try their best to stop the matches from taking place on Saturday. So what they would do was as follows: they would put on their Shabbat clothing, the *kapote*, the long black coat, the *streimel*, a black hat with a rim of thirteen fox-tails, and with the book of psalms in their hands they would walk onto the field. They would stay on the field and say psalms. No one bothered them. Everybody watched, and no one said a word. There was no fighting. After a certain amount of time, they would march off, and the game would start. But as luck would have it, every time they came out to say psalms, our team won. So word spread in camp that the Rabbi and the Chasidim, the followers, were coming out to say psalms for the well-being of the team. After a while, they stopped coming out on the field, and the games went on as scheduled on the Sabbath.

Many, many times, when they finished the match, fights would break out, and literally, police would escort the referee off the field into a car and take him out of the camp because people often thought that this man was paid off and thus made calls against our team on purpose. At times these fights were very ugly. Keep in mind, these were all Jewish people who survived either in death camps or in Siberia or in forests, among other places. One would not have thought that these people could conduct themselves in this way toward each other, but they did. In our camp, we had a number of people that today we would call lowlifes. One was Yankovsky, a Polish Jew from Warsaw, and the other one was called Tzigan, which means gypsy. Tzigan was an extremely powerful man. We had a small jail in camp, and he was arrested once and locked up. That jail had a very heavy iron door on it. He just lifted the iron door off the hinges and walked out of the jail. No one ever bothered him again. Whenever a fight would break out on the field, Tzigan and Yankovsky would take over and walk around moving their hands like scythes, leaving individuals falling on either side of them. It was just like watching a bad movie. It was unbelievable.

In camp, we had enough food. Many times, we received foods that we did not recognize, for example, peanut better. We had never seen that before. We didn't know what to do with certain types of oatmeal that we received. We used to sell them to the Germans or exchange them for fruits or services. My parents had decided that my sister and I should have a little bit more culture. They decided that my sister should take piano lessons, while I should take violin lessons. A piano was difficult to obtain, but a violin was no problem. Obviously, it was not a Stradivarius. And for these lessons, we paid with food. Peanut butter, different kinds of cereals and breads—we had plenty because my father worked in the public kitchen and was able to bring home extra breads that were left over. Once or twice a week, I would go for these private violin lessons. Carrying the violin was sort of embarrassing as far as I was concerned, so therefore, my sister usually carried the violin for me while I rode the new bike that my father bought me in Ginsburg. It was the first time in my life that I owned a bike. I still remember the name of the firm, it was Mars, and I shall never forget that bike as long as I live. And this was how I went to my lesson. On the way back, my sister also carried the violin home while I rode my bike. Of course, if you play violin, you have to practice. Practice makes perfect. So, I practiced two or three times a week, but first there was a ritual I followed. Everyone had to leave the room we all lived in; then I had to cover the window with a blanket to muffle the sound so that no one could hear me and make fun of me. Once everyone was out and the windows were closed and covered, I would practice my violin for about fifteen to twenty minutes. After a number of months, my parents realized that I would never make it as a violinist, and they permitted me to give up this cultural endeavor. My sister, on the other hand, continued to play piano. She played beautifully, and she definitely benefited from it. But unfortunately, I did not.

Seeing Yiddish films was not enough for us. We wanted to see other films, especially American films. For this we had to go to our nearest town, which was Ginsburg, about five or six kilometers away, and there we saw the American films, especially Westerns. These were our favorites. We always walked in groups, no one ever feared for their personal safety, and walking on the roads in Germany was extremely pleasant. All along the roads we had fruit trees, especially apple trees, and we went along and kept on knocking down apples, and we had quite a bit of fun. By 1948, we all practically had bicycles, and it was much easier and even more enjoyable.

As I mentioned earlier, we had a theater in our camp. We also had professional Jewish actors, and they put on all kinds of plays for our camp and for other camps. Sometimes we had performers come from Munich and occasionally, even from the United States. However, to enter the theater we had to purchase tickets. None of the boys worked. We had no money, so we had to improvise a little bit. The theater was a very big building with huge windows all along its back wall. A deep depression a full story high and a fence around the depression to prevent anyone from falling in surrounded the back wall. To access the theater through the window, we had to place a plank from the fence to the window and walk the plank, risking a one-story fall down to basement level. But that didn't stop us. So whenever we wanted to see a play that was showing, a bunch of us would chip in to buy a ticket for one boy to enter the theater the normal way. That young man would then situate himself inside next to one of those windows, while we, on the outside, would prepare the planks. Once the play began, the lights went out and everyone concentrated on the stage and the actors. At that point our friend would open up one or two windows and slowly but surely, each of us, at two- or three-minute intervals, would climb quietly into the theater and very quickly disappear. We were willing to do anything for a little culture. Even when the ushers noticed us, they said nothing, because they did not wish to start a commotion in the theater once the play started. But we had to watch ourselves during intermission, because that was when the ushers came around looking for us. We already knew the drill and mingled with certain crowds to avoid the ushers. At times we were successful; at times we were not so successful and got thrown out during intermission. We always tried to find solutions to problems confronting us. The kids in camp many times proved Herzl right—if there is a will, there is a way.

I stated previously that many illegal transports started from our camp. I recall one morning we woke up and found that American soldiers with jeeps, trucks, and guns had surrounded the entire camp. It seemed that someone had informed the authorities that preparations for a huge transport to Palestine were underway at our camp, and they came to inquire. We were not permitted to leave the barracks. Soldiers walked around with loudspeakers with certain people from camp making the announcements in Yiddish, saying that we were not allowed to leave our barracks, and we should stay away from windows. And I remember one episode where one young boy was looking out from our corridor window. He did not notice that an American soldier ran in. He grabbed that boy by his legs and lowered him from the window as if he were going to drop the boy. It was a strong soldier, and obviously, he just wanted to scare the boy as well as the rest of us away from the windows. He succeeded; we stayed away. The American soldiers did a search of the barracks, and I remember people saying that they were searching for weapons. We were in our barracks when suddenly American soldiers came in. They divided up into pairs. They came to the door, and while one stood with a rifle and a bayonet pointing at us, the other one ran inside, lifted up the mattress, did not even look, and ran out. It seemed as though they were either afraid or just did not care. After half a day of searching, they found no arms. The only thing they found were six cows hidden in a tunnel that were being held for slaughter by black marketeers. Weeks later, the illegal immigration to Palestine continued to leave from our camp.

Every once in a while, we would see American soldiers coming into our camp because in the middle of the camp, there was a communication center that was in military hands. We were too young to know what it was. But there were huge antennas with people listening to something in there. We were not allowed to come too close to that area. It wasn't guarded by anyone outside; perhaps the guards were sitting inside. It was right in the middle of the camp, outside of Block #6, with woods surrounding the house.

I remember one time when there was a black American soldier in the group that came to the communications center. All the kids gathered around him. We admired his dark skin and beautiful white teeth. He was chewing his gum, and he kept on smiling, obviously enjoying every moment of admiration. He spoke to us, but we did not understand him. We thought he was the greatest. That was the first time that any of the kids came face-to-face with a living black person. The only time we had seen a black person was in film.

We children had no contact with the soldiers, but once in a while, these American soldiers would come in, toss pieces of gum or candy to us, and we would run after their truck. That was our contact. However, the adults did have contact with some of them, especially the black marketeers, who would buy nylons, coffee, and cigarettes from the soldiers. These were the main three things that brought in lots of money. And some people, including some soldiers, made large sums of money on the black market. Of course, my father and my uncle never did any of these things. They were straight; they just worked in the kitchen. They were afraid to deal on the black market. And we had no connections to American soldiers.

At the end of 1947 my father discovered another of his cousins was alive. It was Zalman Klitchka from Pritsk. We stayed with them for a short while in 1939. It was there that my sister's hair froze to the headboard. It was where she went to school on a very cold day only to find out that there was no school on that day. This always made an impression on me because something like that could never happen to me. Through Zalman, we found out about Father's cousin, Gishe Greenberg, and through her we found the addresses of Father's second cousin Gishe Apple and her brothers Yisroel and Motl Bichler. We began receiving packages from Gishe Greenberg and a letter from Gishe Apple informing Father that her son, Bernie, was serving in the United States Army in Germany and that he was stationed somewhere in the Nuremberg area. He fell in love with a German girl, and he wrote a letter to his parents that she was Jewish. So his parents wanted my father to check out whether she really was Jewish and to notify them. And of course, if possible, to find out about the family and everything we could learn about her. After a while, my parents received a little note that Bernie would come with the young lady to visit us, and my parents began making preparations. It was a big deal—an American soldier, a cousin, was coming to visit, and that in itself was something extraordinary. My parents spent what was for them a substantial amount of money buying and preparing food. After all, you must welcome him with open arms. Finally, Bernie came to visit my parents. He came with his girlfriend, Elke, and my parents welcomed them into their room. Bernie was very, very tall; Elke was a "nice girl," and he came for the sole purpose of selling my parents on this young lady so they would write a nice letter home to his mother. He was not at all interested in anything about us. He didn't see me. I don't think he saw my sister. The only one he saw was Iris, the little baby. He did not even ask for us. We were in school, and we thought he would spend the day with us. Being that my mother prepared all these special things, he probably thought that we eat that well all the time, and it didn't enter his mind to find out anything about how we live or get on—nothing at all. But meanwhile, in the camp, people began talking and many envied us, because after all, the Bichlers would make it. It was assumed that because we had a cousin in the military he could get us cigarettes, nylons, chocolates, and coffee, and that we would sell it on the black market and earn a fortune—we'd be rich.

The truth of the matter was, he did not bring a single cigarette for Father, a heavy smoker, no coffee, no nylons, not even a piece of chocolate for the baby. He just came in for one purpose: to see my parents so they could send a report. He could not have cared less about us.

Well, Elke was a very nice girl, but the likelihood of her being Jewish was less than slim. She did not look like a camp survivor to them. She was a twenty-two- or twenty-three-year-old pharmacist, and we wondered from what concentration camp university she graduated. My parents did question her about her family, but she had only one answer for everything: they all disappeared. Hitler killed them all; she could not even shed a tear, and she purposely gave names of places that were far from where we lived so that we would have no idea. It was obvious to us that she was hiding her identification. As a human being, she was a nice girl; whether her father and brother were Nazis, we didn't know for certain. There was a good chance that they participated in the slaughter of many, many Jews, but we did not know. So very diplomatically, my parents wrote a letter to Bernie's mother and father, telling them that they met the couple, the son was a very nice young man, and as far as the young lady was concerned, this Elke, they didn't know. She "claimed" that she was Jewish. We lived in a DP Camp, and therefore we had no opportunity to travel around or to investigate whether whatever she was saying was true or not. And we tried to get out of it as diplomatically as possible.

After this encounter with our cousin Bernie, we never saw him nor heard from him again. Obviously he had no interest in us. But to his mother he would write that it was very difficult to be in touch with us being we had no telephone and he was so far away from us. The truth of the matter was that he tried to stay far away from us because otherwise we might have found something out. He didn't realize that we knew all along that she wasn't Jewish. From his mother, on the other hand, we got letters every once in a while, and a package every three or four months. The best packages, we received from Gishe Greenberg. She was very kind. When she sent a package, there were always cigarettes for Father, a couple of pairs of nylons, coffee. She sent all kinds of things that she thought we could sell or use. She was a business lady. She also was better off than the others. Gishe Apple, on the other hand, was a very poor lady. We used to look forward to receiving a package. This was one of my highlights. This was what we dreamed of—a package from America. Part of my responsibility was to check the bulletin board every day in the camp center, where a printed list of the names of those people who received packages was displayed. If your name was on the list, you would have to go to the central post office to claim your package.

I remember one episode. One boy from our town, the *Lange Itze* (the Tall Itze) who could hardly spell his name, came in to my parents one evening and said he was running through the center of camp and noticed our name was listed for a package. My father called me in and was ready to kill me: "How dare you not check? Where is your responsibility?" So I rushed over to the center to check and, of course, our name was not listed. I knew it wouldn't be because every day, I would go religiously, to check to make sure not to miss our names on the list. Meanwhile, I was accused of having interest only in playing soccer, not caring about the well-being of the family, and always just worrying for myself. After this episode, I think my father realized that I did check every day, and I was responsible, and he took my word for it after that.

It was May 1948—May fourteenth was approaching, and the camp attached loudspeakers to telephone poles and trees, especially in the center. Certain areas were decorated in preparations for the declaration of independence of the State of Israel. People in the camp knew what was taking place in Palestine. Months and months before that, people were glued to their radios. We knew of the terrorist actions that the Arabs were committing. We knew of the people that were killed. We listened to the radio. We were very well informed of what was taking place in Palestine and at the United Nations. Finally, the day came. Hundreds if not thousands of people concentrated in the center of the camp. It was May 14, 1948, the fifth day of the Hebrew month of Iyar in the year 5708. We heard the proclamation of Israel by David Ben Gurion, ". . . do hereby proclaim the establishment of a Jewish state in the land of Israel—the State of Israel."

Old people were crying; younger ones were singing and dancing. We the survivors are the most cursed and at the same time the most blessed generation in Jewish history. Our generation survived the most atrocious crimes ever committed against people in the history of mankind. And at the same time we lived to see the establishment of the Jewish State after two thousand years of exile, degradation, humiliation, discrimination, pogroms, expulsions, and almost total extermination.

The singing, dancing, and crying of joy lasted for hours. It was like electricity going through the camp. The camp was never the same after that. It's a well-known fact that as soon as Israel proclaimed its independence, all its surrounding Arab neighbors declared war on her. And in our camp, a mobilization was begun. The equivalent of draft boards were set up in the DP Camps, and every boy and girl that was single, eighteen and older, had to register with this draft board. These boys and girls were sent away either to Israel or to other places for training. Some said they got their basic training in Italy; I don't know. But they were sent away. Any young lady or young man who did not report to this draft board was pretty much ostracized. It was known more or less who didn't register, and they were blacklisted. They weren't permitted to go into a movie or the theater. People would look at them and sometimes even spit in their direction because they were looked upon as traitors. There was quite a bit of tension in the camp.

We, in our room, had a radio that enabled us to receive the broadcasts from Israel. Therefore, every evening, many of the other people would gather in our room. One of the people there was *Shmiel-Goidl* (the Big Samuel). He was from our town, and his son was one of boys who was drafted. He was a brilliant young guy. Under different circumstances, this young man could have been a great inventor, or great engineer, or actually, anything he really wanted. He had golden hands and an excellent mind. All these people gathered in our room and listened to the broadcast from Israel. You could hear a pin drop in our room. Most of the time, even before the broadcast, they would kick the kids out because they did not want any interference. And this went on for months. Day in and day out, evenings were dedicated to this purpose. This went on until the first cease-fire, I believe. It went on for months and months.

Things began changing. There was no more illegal immigration from our camp. Suddenly everything was legal. Every day we watched our friends or neighbors pack up, gather everything they had, and go to Israel. Suddenly, the camp was a temporary place, no longer a permanent residence, and there was a very strange feeling, especially for the kids. I assume that the adults always thought of the camp as a transit area, but to us kids, it was sort of a permanent situation. Suddenly, this permanent life took on a tremendous change.

Twenty-Three

People suddenly began thinking about what they would do in Israel. How would they make a living? And I remember, my uncle and my father, at that time, could not decide whether we should go to Israel or to America. I believe, by then, we already had received our affidavits from my father's cousin Motl Bichler stating that he would be responsible for us and that we would not be a burden upon the United States government, and we registered for immigration to America. But we did not really believe that this would actually happen. It was not an easy matter because our family and my uncle's family, with Grandma, had not been separated from each other from the moment we were taken by force from Poland in 1939. And suddenly, after surviving this terrible Holocaust, it was difficult to think that we would separate. On the other hand, my father was practically all alone. He was the sole survivor of his family. He did find three cousins here and there, but somehow he thought that these cousins in America would be closer family because he remembered them from when they went to the United States, and he thought it would be the same. He found out later that it was very different. But with all this, we still thought that going to Israel was a real possibility. So my uncle and my father and other people began to think about what they would do in Israel when they got there. And they used to sit and discuss this. Being that my uncle was a master builder, one of their ideas was to buy a small cement-mixing machine and with this, my uncle and my father could work together and have sustenance for the families. Other people thought of the same thing or other types of machinery that they could bring in to help them establish themselves in Israel and start new lives for themselves and their families.

In the meantime, the Americans came in and blew up the airfield that was right outside our camp, creating craters of various sizes. We used to ride bikes there because it was not used by planes, except once in a while, German youths used to come there with gliders just to fly around a little bit. They damaged it so badly that it was impossible to ride our bikes. Then rumors started that the Americans were beginning to pack up and leave Germany. I don't know from where people got these rumors. And meanwhile, more and more people began leaving the camp for Israel. And those people who had ideas of going to America, Canada, Australia, or other places remained. As time went on, the American authorities suddenly came in and announced that our camp was going to be closed down. I think it was the beginning of 1949. Suddenly they came back and began to rebuild the airfield, which they blew up a number of months earlier. We just couldn't figure out for the life of us what was going on.

Then we learned that the Americans were going to turn Leipheim into an air force base, and all the remaining people in Leipheim were to be moved to a new camp, that is, an existing camp by the name of Neu-Ulm. It was roughly twenty miles away from Leipheim. It was near Ulm on the Dunhau, the city where Albert Einstein was born. When we came to Neu-Ulm, we were given a room, and near us, my grandma and uncle had a room, but it was never the same as it was in Leipheim. We were not registered to go to school anymore; we were sort of sitting on our valises. Quite a number of people from there packed up and left for Israel. And quite a number went to other countries. Suddenly, my uncle began thinking that maybe he too should think about going to America in order to keep the family together. But he was not certain; he didn't know what to do even though the idea was in his mind.

My friends and I went to a trade school for about two months or so. I learned how to operate textile machines. I do not remember what my sister did, but father did not work there. Life was totally different than in Leipheim. The people from Leipheim tried to stick together. They felt like relatives, and they had very little in common with the people in Ulm. We even felt strange in the synagogue there. The kids from Leipheim tried to stick together as well. On the Sabbath, we would go walking into the city of Ulm, and sometimes we would even go to see a match there. We were able to see the German league play because Ulm was a member; I think the soccer team was Ulm 46. We also tried to go to a movie in Ulm itself, but it was quite different. We practically never associated with the other kids of Neu-Ulm. We were always the Leipheim kids, and we were always together. We felt that we really were removed from home. When we walked around in Ulm, we couldn't help but notice the huge parts of Ulm that were bombed out by the massive bombings of the Allies. But one thing though, the cathedral, stood unharmed. And we wondered how it was possible for the planes to do such a nice job of preserving this church when they couldn't do anything to knock out the railroads or the gas chambers. When I speak about the railroads, I'm talking about the railroads leading into the death camps. I don't think it's that they couldn't. The order was never given, and nobody gave a darn about the Jews. That was the feeling that we all had.

When we registered to go to America, we had great doubts whether our dream would be fulfilled. We were Polish Jews, and we had to go under the quota allotted from Poland. The Polish quota, like the quota of other eastern European countries, was slow moving. The reason was that for many years the United States considered Eastern European immigrants inferior. Historians in America traditionally referred to the Europeans who came before 1890 as "Old Immigrants." They originated chiefly from Great Britain, Ireland, Germany, Holland, France, Denmark, Norway, and Sweden. They came while the frontier was still open, and many settled on farms in the West.

The Europeans who came after 1890 were referred to as "New Immigrants." They came in greater numbers and originated chiefly in Italy, Greece, Austria-Hungary, Serbia, Rumania, Russian-Poland, and Russia. They arrived when the frontier was closed and settled mainly in the cities as factory workers. Many people in America argued that the "New Immigrants" were physically and mentally inferior to the "Old Immigrants." This was known as the "Theory of Nordic Supremacy." As a result of this theory, many acts were passed restricting the "New Immigrants." In 1921 the Emergency Quota Act limited the annual number of immigrants from each nation to three percent of foreign-born persons residing in the United States from that nation according to the 1910 census.

In 1924 the Immigration Act passed and reduced immigration quotas to two percent and shifted the base date to 1890, thereby favoring the "Old Immigrants." This act also contained more permanent regulations, which became the National Origins Plan. The following are regulations from the National Origins Plan of 1929, which:

- allowed no more than one hundred fifty thousand immigrants from outside the Western Hemisphere to enter the United States per year;
- allotted each country a quota in proportion to the number of persons in the U.S. having that national origin according to the census of 1910;
- granted each eligible nation at least one hundred immigrants per year;
- placed no restrictions on immigration from the Western Hemisphere; and
- prohibited all immigration from Asian countries.

But what happened was that in 1947, the United States Congress passed the Displaced Persons Act, permitting two hundred fifty thousand refugees above the yearly immigration quota to come in to the United States. All in all, the United States passed several Displaced Persons Acts, which allowed some six hundred thousand refugees into the United States by 1956. In the beginning of 1949, we saw that more and more people from the camp were permitted to go to the United States. The American government began posting lists of people in Augsburg. Every ten days to two weeks a new list would be posted, and if your name was on that list, you would have to appear before the military intelligence, where they would especially interrogate the parents. And that was the beginning of the process. It was in March or April that I began making weekly or biweekly trips to Augsburg to see if our names were on the list. And finally, finally by the beginning of May, our name appeared, and then things were happening.

My father began worrying very much. What should he tell them if he was interrogated? Should he tell the truth? Should he not tell the truth? Should he tell the truth that we were in Russia, Siberia, Asia, or should he lie and say that we were hidden someplace by peasants or we were in the forests? He was worried that if he said that we were in Russia, they might think that we were Communists and therefore not permit us to enter the United States. So for nights, the poor man did not sleep. He began talking to other people and seeking advice, and every person had a different story and a different thing to tell him. He got so carried away and was so afraid that he ripped up all the pictures he had of himself as a soldier in the Polish army in the very early '30s, because G-d knows what the American Intelligence might think of him. The fact that Poland was a democracy at that time did not enter his mind at all. He destroyed everything. And this went on, like a punishment, for weeks until we were called out. And when we were called out for the interrogation, we were told that only Father and Mother had to come; the children did not. Before they knew that children would not be questioned they used to tell us, remember, don't say this and don't say that. You're not listening, you're not paying attention, be very careful. It was just unbelievable. And finally, when the moment came and my father and mother were in there, my father decided that the best way was the truth—he was not going to start lying, and what happened would happen. And when he told them that we were in Russia from 1939 to 1945, they asked where we were, and my father told them about the Taiga and the Ural mountains in Siberia, Asia. The only thing these people wanted to know is how we managed to survive, and they only wanted to hear what he did there, not because they worried that he was a Communist but because of the interest in what this man went through. And when he came out of there, he was a newborn person. The truth paid off.

Then we had to make preparations to report with the entire family to Augsburg. The entire family would have to undergo physicals, and once we passed the physicals, we would be able to come to the Promised Land. I must confess that we all walked around, especially I, in a daze. I don't think I thought of anyone.

The only thing we thought of, or I thought of, was America, and G-d knows what I would be able to do when I got to America. All these things that we heard about America and all these things that we saw in the movies about America were suddenly going to be possible to accomplish. America was like a magnet. No one knew what really lay ahead. We expected that the streets were literally paved with gold and silver, and we could just bend down and pick it up. Yes, I had great illusions about how things would be easy and wonderful in this mighty, mighty, rich country. We were so overwhelmed, we didn't even think about breaking up the family. Nothing. We only saw America in front of our eyes.

There was one man with us in Neu-Ulm from our town by the name of Shtimer Luzar (Luzar the Stammerer), who lived in the States in the early '30s and came back home. He would laugh when he heard us speak about America, with the streets paved with gold, and he would say, "Wait until you work in the sweat shops." But we did not understand what he was saying. He went to Israel.

And the good day came when our family was notified that we had to report to Augsburg, so everything was packed up, whatever we had, in one crate and a valise or two, and we reported to Augsburg. There we had barracks, and we were given part of a room, with cots to sleep on, and we awaited the medical examination. The main doctor was a German doctor whose name I shall never forget. He was Dr. Kruger. And he had to sign, and if he signed that you were okay, you were able to come to America. Father, both of my sisters, and I passed the physical, but my mother somehow failed the physical because this Dr. Kruger misread her lung x-ray. He thought she had something on her lungs. The first thing we did, we ran to the HIAS (Hebrew Immigrant Aid Society) and asked for help. In the HIAS there was a man by the name Spitzer. He arranged to send my mother to another doctor. The other doctor looked and didn't see anything wrong with

Mother. But once Dr. Kruger said there was something wrong, he couldn't go back on his word. The HIAS promised that within the year Mother would join us in America.

We did not know what to do, but as I mentioned before, the name America had tremendous pull, and we were so blinded, and I must say, especially I, that we decided to go to America and that Mother would come a year later. There were two reasons for this decision. First of all, we were blinded by the magic of America. Secondly, we felt that we were not leaving Mother alone. My grandmother and my uncle and his family were still there, and since Mother could stay with them, it was not as though we left her all alone. That was our logic in leaving my mother behind. But I'm just wondering if we would have left Mother had my uncle not still been there. And, I dare say, we probably would have, because the magic of America was so powerful that we would have probably found another convincing reason.

Once we made this decision, we came back to Augsburg for about one week. We were in big rooms together with other families. Across from our beds was another family. That family's name was Nussman, and they were from our camp. The Nussman's had one son who was extremely ill; he couldn't stand on his feet, and he was going to America too. This Mr. Nussman tried to justify somehow his son's ability to go to America, so he constantly carried with him a lung x-ray that he showed everyone and said, "Look how clear my son's lungs are; look how beautiful they are." As if anyone there was capable of reading x-rays. At the same time that we were there, there was also that Yankovsky, whom I mentioned earlier. Somehow he failed the physical. He was a giant and as strong as an ox. He used to come around to our room because he knew us from Leiphem, but more so, it killed him to see that this sick guy was going to America and he had to sit out a few weeks and wait for Dr. Kruger to decide his fate. So Mr. Yankovsky would come whenever he needed a few dollars or marks at that time, and he would make a speech: "Look at this sick person over there. He is going to America, but I, who can pick them all up with one arm, am lying in this basket. I cannot go to America. Where is the justice? How much did you pay for this x-ray that you carry around?" Obviously Mr. Nussman did not like to hear this. He was afraid. He knew that this Yankovsky was speaking the truth. So he would give him a few marks to shut him up and make him leave. Every couple of days Mr. Yankovsky needed a few marks, and he would show up and make his speech and get what he wanted. We watched, listened, laughed, and enjoyed the moment. It made it easier for us to forget our own troubles. Thus, we learned that it was possible to pay these doctors, including maybe Kruger and the people around him. When you paid up, they would take x-rays from healthy people and switch them, but by the time we found this out it was too late, and even if it hadn't been too late, we did not have the amount of money that was necessary for this bribery. Some individuals did have it.

In our blindness and our great desire to come to America, we forgot that my little sister was only about four years old and would have to be away from Mother for a long time. We also didn't think about the rough time we all would have being separated from Mother and the sufferings that this would cause for our mother. Had we known at the time what we learned later, we would never, ever have separated from Mother, even if it had meant not coming to the United States. But, wisdom came a little too late. We did what we did because we thought it was the best for everyone, and soon we were on our way to Brehmenhaven, where we stayed for a little less than a week before embarkation on our way to the United States.

In Brehmenhaven, we stayed in an American military camp. Every morning, we heard the bugle, and we had to stand at attention when they raised the American flag and again in the evening when they lowered it. The accommodations were decent. Everybody had a nice, clean cot to sleep on. There was a cafeteria where they served us three meals a day. There were no other people that we knew; no one from our camp was there at that time. The great majority of the people in the camp were not Jews but Ukrainians, and they were running away, or so they said, because they did not wish to live under the Communist government. But we had our suspicions that many, if not most, of these Ukrainians were going to America for different reasons. A few of them, very few, did not participate with the Germans against the Jews. Many ran away because they were afraid that they might be brought to justice. Many of them robbed from Jews, many participated in killing Jews, and many collaborated with the Germans against the Russians as well as numerous other things. And then, a large number of them decided to go to the United States. Suddenly they were great lovers of freedom and believed in the dignity of human beings. They walked around the camp smiling and very courteously spoke to my father; they behaved like totally different human beings. They knew we were Jewish, and the hypocrisy of these people was very evident, but there was nothing one could do.

It was on June 28 or 29 that the embarkation took place. We sailed on a military transport ship by the name of *General Blechford*. We were hundreds and hundreds of people on this boat. We all stood in cabins below deck. My father and I were in a huge cabin with about 350 people. There were cots, but they were one above the other, three high. My father was on the lowest, I was on the middle, and there was one man above me. It looked more like a hospital than a cabin on a ship. My sisters were in different cabins, but truthfully speaking, neither of them was in their cabin for too long, because they did not feel well on the ship. To be more correct, they were extremely seasick during the entire journey.

Our hearts went out to them. They just couldn't take the sailing on the ocean.

On board the boat there was a huge cafeteria, but there was no sitting room. You came in, took a tray with a plate etc., and followed the line as they served you whatever there was that day; then you would walk over to a table, where you'd eat while standing. When done, you would deposit your tray and cutlery for washing at a designated place and you'd walk out. We were fed three times a day. The first day, I remember, all of us went into the cafeteria. But after that, my sisters never saw the inside of the cafeteria again. My father and I, however, went to eat three times a day, and whenever there was something good or something that would be good for my sisters such as a pickle or fruit, anything we could get our hands on, we would bring it for them. We were told that if you ate, you felt better, and you would not suffer so much from the seasickness.

It was interesting to watch these Ukrainians on the boat. Strong, healthy guys would stay in the line, get their food, and eat the food together with us there in standing position. Not too far after you walked out, there were barrels, and you would see them standing and vomiting into the barrels. They just could not hold the food down. But my father and I did not suffer any seasickness at all. Our worries were only my sisters, and not the seasickness. This we could cope with. Every time my father and I finished eating, we went on deck to be with my sisters and to help them as much as we could. Of course, it was particularly hard for my sister Bracha, who not only felt ill, but also had to be the so-called mother for my little four-year-old sister, Chaya. We tried to get fruits for them when possible, but unfortunately we were not given many fruits. For some reason the crew members were saving them; possibly, they were saving the oranges and the grapefruits for the Fourth of July celebration. One day, we were on deck, and we saw that they threw overboard what seemed like hundreds of cases of citrus fruit that rotted. Had they not have saved them, and given them out sooner, we would surely have enjoyed them.

Sometimes a sailor would pass by, a nice guy, and if he would see somebody not feeling well, especially a young child, he would bring out a fruit. But this did not happen too many times. One day, they began talking about a storm approaching. No one was allowed on the deck, and that was terrible for us. We couldn't be with my sisters, and they both were extremely seasick. But everybody had to be on his or her cot in the cabins. The doors were tied down, and a storm did approach. It was a vicious storm. As a matter of fact, a man not far from us lying on top fell down and almost broke his neck. We were all laughing, but it wasn't really a laughing matter. The guy who fell down did not laugh, but the people around had nothing better to do, so we were laughing and saying thank G-d it was not us. Our worry was only, of course, my sisters, because this was a ferocious storm. But the morning right after the storm, we came out on the deck and saw them and thanked G-d they survived. They were just as sick during the storm as before the storm and then after the storm. For them, nothing changed.

I loved this sailing on the boat very much. I loved to watch the sea, the waves; everything looked so straight on a calm day. Beautiful. We were able to see the fish jumping out of the waters. It was a magnificent thing to see, and once in a while you would see another ship sailing quite far away. Land, we never saw. We thought, that's it, we'll never see land again, because when you're on an ocean, you think somehow that the land has disappeared. But all in all, it was just magnificent. The ocean was beautiful, especially the sunrise and sunset. Those are the most beautiful times to be on a boat, but of course, under good circumstances, and not under our circumstances. On the one hand, we were extremely happy to be going to the United States; on the other hand, we were unhappy because our family was split up.

The announcements on the boat were made in Polish, Ukrainian, and also in English. We, of course, understood the Polish and the Ukrainian or the Russian, whatever the case was. Each person on the boat was given coupons worth five dollars, I believe. And with this, we were able to buy whatever we wanted in the ship's cantina. I remember we went down to the cantina and the first thing my father bought was cigarettes—Pall Mall because they were the longest—and he bought some other things too. I got myself a Butterfinger. I'll never forget that Butterfinger. We got a box of them. Of course, we tried to get something for my sisters. I don't remember whether we got something for them or not, because they couldn't eat sweets; they couldn't even look at them without getting sick. I opened up the Butterfinger, and when I ate it, I was sure that there was nothing in the world better than that Butterfinger. I still remember the taste today, and to this day it is one of my favorite candy bars.

We did not have entertainment on the boat. Our entertainment was to listen to the mispronounced announcements. Most of the time the announcements were made by some crew members on board, and sometimes their usage of Polish and Russian would make us crack up. One announcement I still remember. As we were coming closer to the shore, we began to see Boston Harbor in the distance. We saw the city's skyline, and as everybody rushed out on the decks to see it, the announcement came on. The announcer wanted to say that all the people should return to their own cabins; instead, he announced, ". . . every person should return to his own toilet." People were cracking up, and the crew just looked at us, not understanding why we were laughing so hard. They couldn't understand what was going on. If they had known what they were saying, I think they, too, would have been laughing. Of course, finally we understood what he wanted to say, and everybody had to go down, because it was evening when we came to the shores of the

United States, and they would not permit our ship to dock in the evening. We had to remain in our cabins on the ship until the following morning when we pulled into Boston Harbor.

Twenty-Four

It was July 7, 1949 that we came into the harbor. Everybody was extremely happy, exalted. After all, we had reached the Promised Land. We all had one hope, and one hope only—that the Promised Land would be what we imagined it to be. We all wanted a new life in the new world, a life where we would not fear to practice our religion; a life where we would have enough to eat and to drink and freely walk the streets; a life where we could educate the children and do as we please. That was our hope and desire.

Our first glance at Boston was a little disappointing. The area where the boat docked looked quite bad. Many people were a little disillusioned by their first glance of America. We hoped that this was not the true picture of America, and it surely was not.

After a number of hours of waiting on the ship with the few things that we had, we were finally given permission to disembark. When we got off, everybody was moving around, looking for his or her belongings. We had a small crate, and when we finally found the crate we went back in line with it and a few other belongings. They opened up our crate and began checking, and once they looked in they didn't have to look very much. They saw a few feather blankets, a few other shmattes in there, and they very quickly closed it and sent us on our way.

Of course we were all very tense and very nervous. It's one thing to look forward to coming to America. It's another thing coming into a new country, not knowing what is awaiting you, and we did not know what Boston meant, or New York, or anything else. We only hoped that there would be someone waiting for us.

As we got out, my father's cousin Motl, with his son Alan, were standing there waiting for us. They managed to put everything into their car, and we were on our way. We saw that Motl was very ill. It was quite easy to speak to my father's cousin Motl; he spoke Yiddish. Of course, he would throw in English words. But his son Alan neither understood nor spoke a word of Yiddish.

We made our journey from Boston to the area where we were going to live. It was Sullivan County, between Monticello and Port Jervis. Motl owned a small hotel there. It was called Pine Grove Lodge. On our way from Boston (that took probably about four hours or so) we stopped a number of times, and each time, I remember they gave us ice cream soda. It was very delicious. I don't think I had ever had ice cream soda before. If we had gotten ice cream, we surely never would have put the ice cream into the soda. But we were in America, and it was delicious. The first time we got the ice cream soda we saw a napkin and a straw next to the glass. We had never seen straws before. And we did not know what to do with them. My sister was watching Alan to see what he was doing. But he took his time, maybe to see what we would do. Finally he took the straw and put it into the soda, and my sister did the same. I did not use the straw at all. I drank the soda and ate the ice cream. And when we arrived to that little hotel, we were the main attraction. Everybody awaited us, not only the family, but also the guests in the hotel. Everyone knew that we were coming, and everyone was there to welcome us. Of course, there was my cousin's wife Pauline, and she spoke Yiddish. Her youngest son Blair and the older daughter Florence and her two children were there; the younger daughter Susan was there. Their older son, Myron, was not there, but came a week or two later to see us. Many people were able to speak to us in Yiddish; however, in their immediate family, only Motl and his wife Pauline spoke Yiddish fluently. The rest neither spoke it nor understood it. Perhaps I should also mention, they had a dog by the name of Prince who was also there to welcome us.

The first evening that we were there and sat down to eat, everybody watched us; they walked around looking at us as if we were from another planet. They were amazed at our ability to use forks and knives correctly. Then they showed us to our room. They put us all together in one room and then waited for us to unpack. Everybody in the family wanted to see the great things that we brought to America. We were sort of embarrassed to unpack, but we had to unpack and take the stuff out of that crate, and finally we did. When they saw what we brought, I think they lost their appetites. They didn't want to watch. They only saw the beginning, and that was sufficient. However, we did bring a beautiful gift for them; we brought sterling silverware, service for twelve. We paid a lot of money for it, and we thought it was magnificent. We gave it to Pauline; she took it and didn't show it to anyone. And I don't think anyone knew that we gave them a gift. It bothered us a little, but of course we couldn't say anything.

The people there were quite nice. A number were old-time Europeans, like Pauline's father who was there, Mr. Pfeffer. He spoke Yiddish beautifully. He was in the States perhaps fifty years, and he was a very nice fellow. He played cards every day. There were other families there too. There was the Pomerantz family, I remember. Mr. Pomerantz was a bus driver, I found out later. There was the Schaeffer family from the Bronx. With them we spoke Yiddish a little bit. Schaeffer had a son about my age who spoke a little Hebrew because he went to a Talmud Torah, so with him I was able to exchange a few more words, and I walked with him more than I ever did with my cousin who did not know a single word in another language.

What amazed me was to watch some of the people. They really made impressions on me that I can remember until this day. On Friday evening, Mrs. Schaeffer and Mrs. Pomerantz lit Shabbat candles—and then each would take out a cigarette and light it from the Shabbat candles. To me, that was not only bizarre, but also a terrible thing to do. We looked and said: "Wow, only in America do you see a thing like that."

There was not much for us to do in that small hotel. My sister began cleaning the rooms, straightening out the beds, but there weren't too many, and once in a while she would get a dollar tip. I think she would get the tip more because they felt sorry for us there than for the work. My father would try to do something here and there, but there was not much to do because there were very few guests in the hotel. But my cousin Motl had plans for us. He had lots of acreage and was in the process of building a chicken farm for us to take care of and earn a good living.

However, his wife and kids—especially his daughter Florence—tried to counteract every move that Motl made. And rightfully so; he was a very sick person and did not want to realize that. I remember one night, watching through our window as they paid off the worker to leave. He got into his car, but they didn't let him start the engine because they were afraid it would make too much noise. They pushed the car out of the driveway and started the engine only after the car was on the road. The guy took off and never came back, and that was the end of the chicken coops.

Then Motl talked about setting up Father with a Jewish baker in Port Jervis. He took Father around a little bit, but he couldn't get around well and nothing came of that idea either. Had Motl not been so sick, our situation would have been totally different. He tried, but it was physically too difficult for him. Motl was convinced that if we went into the city and my father started working in a factory, he would always work very hard for very little. Sadly, that turned out to be too true.

Meanwhile in Germany, Mother was sent to be tested by another doctor and then was sent to a sanitarium, I think in Hindenlang, for over two months. The head of the sanitarium was at one time Dr. Kruger's teacher. After undergoing tests for tuberculosis, reports were sent to Dr. Kruger that there was nothing wrong with her lungs, and she was discharged from the sanitarium. At this time Neu-Ulm camp was closed down. Uncle realized that there was no chance for his family to come to America, so he opted to go to Israel and not make another move to a third DP Camp. Mother, all alone with no choice, moved to a new DP Camp by the name of Lechtfeld while she was waiting to be reunited with us. She suffered greatly being all alone. Mother missed the family and especially the baby very much. She used to cry herself to sleep most of the nights. We certainly were longing for her and felt miserable and guilty for leaving her alone. We in America did not lick honey either.

Most of the time at my cousins', we were hungry, and it was probably not their fault. The reason for it was that when we sat down to eat together with them, we ate what they served us, but we were embarrassed to ask for seconds. We ate what we got, and that was it. The kitchen was always open there, and the others would go into the kitchen and take whatever they wanted whenever they wanted. We did not dare to go into the kitchen, and none of them thought about encouraging us or giving us things or calling us to eat and so on. So we were walking around hungry many times. And as I mentioned, my sister would make a few dollars in tips. And once or twice a week, the bread truck would come in early, and my sister would go over and for a dollar or so buy one or two Tip-Top breads to take upstairs to our room. And this helped us a great deal; when we were hungry, we would grab a piece or two of this bread. A little bit later, I found a pecan tree, and I collected a lot of these nuts and brought them to the room. And this also helped us a little.

On the premises, there was a casino and jukebox and all kinds of things, and in the evening, they would play there and sometimes dance. My cousin Alan was an excellent dancer, and girls who lived in the area and from surrounding hotels would come there just to dance. There was a refrigerator loaded with ice creams, and every time I passed by, my mouth would water. My cousins would go over and take an ice cream pop and just eat, but they never bothered offering me one, because they no doubt thought that if I wanted an ice cream, I would go over and take one just as they did. But we were never comfortable doing that. I believe an ice cream was either a nickel or a dime, but I had neither the nickel nor the dime Every once in a while, I must admit, if no one was around, I would go in there, take an ice cream out, wrap it in a napkin, put it in my pocket, and go away someplace in the bushes and eat it. And I enjoyed every moment of it. My only problem was I couldn't bring one to my sisters or my father. I believe one person knew what I was doing, and that was the old man Mr. Pfeffer, Pauline's father. He would smile; he never said a word about it to me or to anyone. I am positive he knew, but I'm sure it didn't bother him because he knew that we were talking about a dime or a nickel, and I would do that maybe, maybe, once or twice a week. I can't recall anymore, but not more than that. I am positive that had my cousins thought about it, they would have given my sisters and me the ice cream any time. I am sure it was not the cost that bothered them. They just did not think about it. They never put themselves in our position, and that is why we walked around hungry without them ever being aware of it.

Alan on the other hand, once a week, once every two weeks, would take us to a movie to Port Jervis. My sister would go once in a while, but most of the time he would take me to Port Jervis, and we'd get to see a Western film. He would buy me popcorn or something to drink; whatever he bought for himself, he bought for me. However, whenever I went to see the films, a few things bothered me. Number one, whenever we walked in, the film was already playing, the double features. In Europe this never happened. You had to go in when the film began, you stayed until the end, you walked out, there was a certain time to clean, and then they would come back and the next group of people would enter. Here, it was continuous. And the second thing that bothered me a lot was I could not comprehend how people could sit, eat, drink, and watch how those Indians were being killed. Everyone was shooting at them. They were falling off their horses left and right, and the people kept on sitting, eating, and drinking. After going through World War II, this was very strange to me. How can you enjoy yourself while you watch somebody being killed? I was not used to it. It was very bizarre. It took me a number of years to get used to the idea that here, killing the Indians was nothing; it was an Indian, not a human being. It was almost like a Jew to a German—except I never saw Indian children or women being shot, just warriors. I had great difficulty with this concept. It always amazed me how a guy with a six-shooter could kill so many Indians. And we used to sit watching these double features for hours. We would come in the middle and we would leave in the middle. It was an amazing thing to me. Very amazing and very strange.

Life was quite difficult, especially for my father, my older sister, and my younger sister. They missed Mother; the little one missed Mother very, very much. She did not understand these people. She did not know the people. She would hold on to us for dear life, and they just could not understand why this child was so attached to us, especially to my big sister. They wanted her to run around and play and feel free. They were just too ignorant to understand the mind of a little one, a four-and-a-half-year-old child. They just couldn't understand, and they began making fun of her, calling her nicknames, all kinds of silly things, and these things made her resent them even more and caused her to be even more attached to my sister and father. They kept saying, how will you ever go to work? What are you going to do with her? What's wrong with this child? What's the matter with this child? It got to the point where they would sometimes get very angry, especially Motl. He was a sick man and had no tolerance, and he took his frustrations out on this child. It bothered us a great deal, but there was nothing we could do about it.

At one point, our cousins got together and decided to Americanize us. They began changing our names. First of all, our family name was no longer going to be Bichler; it was going to be Bickler, because after all, a lot of Americans couldn't pronounce Bichler. They pronounced it "Bitch-ler," and it wasn't nice, so we had to change it to Bickler. My name, Abraham, they changed to Arthur. Then as a middle name, even though I already had two middle names of my own, they added on Otto, totally German. My father's name was Solomon, which they left but called him Sol. My sister's name, Bracha, they changed to Beryl. My little sister Chaya's name they changed to Clair, which she positively hated because one of the hotel guests had a Mexican Chihuahua he called Clair. And so it was—they and all the hotel guests began calling us by these new names. I don't remember whether it bothered us or not, but I don't think we knew what was going on. We were sort of dazed. We did not understand the language. My sister was the only one who understood a little bit and was able to speak a little. They used to sit around for hours discussing these things, without asking us anything. They were just making plans on how to integrate us, so to speak, or how to make us more American without really learning the language or anything else. They were making plans for us. The more I think about it, the more I see how they wanted to run away from Jewish things, especially with the names. Here we were, people who just survived the horrible Holocaust. Why did they have to pick German names for me? They should have been a little bit more sensitive. If Abraham was good enough for President Lincoln, it was good enough for me. But I don't think they thought about how it made us feel to be given German names. They just thought that they were the ones who knew everything and we were just greenhorns and knew very little, so they decided to do the thinking for us.

Suddenly the summer came to an end. Now I know what it was—it was Labor Day. And the day after, everyone packed up and left the countryside. Then we really had a problem. We were the only ones in the hotel. There was no one to speak to. The other hotels in the area were the same. Every hotel was empty. It was a summer resort, and the summer was over. They were locked up for the winter. My cousins had a winter home on their property. Their married daughter went back to New York; only our cousin and his wife and three children remained.

We realized that our problem was even greater than we thought. Our mistake was in not immigrating through the HIAS. Had we come through the HIAS like so many others, we would have been placed in New York City, and they would have found us housing and jobs and given us food. But we entered on our cousin's affidavit.

The school year was starting, and they registered me at the Monticello High School. Every day, my cousin Blair, three other kids, and I were driven to school in a seven-passenger DeSoto. It was a big school with what seemed to me like thousands of students. I was put into classes and had no idea what was going on. Only in math was I able to participate. I walked around in school without talking. I believe it was the principal who came to say a few words to me almost every day because he spoke German. He was a very nice man. The students were also nice. Once I was standing on line for lunch. I noticed through the window girls playing soccer. I was in shock. I remained standing because never before had I seen girls playing my favorite sport. The line moved up, and I returned to the end of the line just so I could watch them play. Some students noticed and brought me back to my place on line. As I said, they were all very nice.

Twenty-Five

For Father and my sister it was getting worse. They had nothing to do but look at the walls. Motl did not speak to his sister or brother, but his sister, Gishe, kept on calling us once or twice a week. In October she called us and asked us to come and stay with her. Motl was furious, but we decided to go to New York. Gishe sent a taxi for us. We put everything in the taxi and moved to New York. Pauline was very pleased with our decision, but not Motl. After about two hours we arrived to the South Bronx on Wilkins Avenue where she lived. Gishe, her husband, Sam, and their two teenagers lived in a two-bedroom apartment on the third floor of a walk-up building. They had a television; it was the first time in our lives that we saw one, and we were awestruck. At their home it was different; we immediately felt comfortable. They were traditional like us, our young cousins spoke Yiddish and a little Hebrew, and we were able to communicate effortlessly. We very much appreciated what they did for us; although they were poor with little enough room for themselves, they took us in and were ready to help us.

That Friday night and Saturday morning we went to the synagogue for the first time since we arrived to America. The Rabbi N. Chodesh welcomed us and asked where we lived. We told him our story. He told us that there was an apartment in his building at 885 Jennings Street. He offered to help us get it, and he delivered on his promise. We got an apartment above a store in the middle of the fruit market. We were very happy, even though it was very noisy and smelly. The good part was that the rooms were nice and the people in the market spoke Yiddish. The monthly rent was twenty-eight dollars, and getting the money was not easy. For the first month we borrowed from Gishe. Father immediately got a part-time job plucking chickens, but it paid very little. Within a week or two we met some people, and Beatrice got a job in a millinery factory making ladies' hats. We also pawned off Father's gold watch that we had buried in Siberia for one hundred dollars to Mother's second cousin. Within two to three weeks I got a job in a factory that made ladies' handbags (Max Weinman Inc.). It was right near the HIAS and entailed carrying cut plastic from the sixth to the fourth floor, all day, for seventy-five cents an hour. Slowly but surely we began earning enough to pay the rent and buy food.

In February of 1950 Mother arrived to New York. It was freezing outside, but we were very warm on the inside. There was no end to our joy. We were finally a united family again. Within a short period of time Father found a full-time job in a factory; Mother worked part time in a bakery across the street from our building so that she could care for Iris. We paid back the money we borrowed and redeemed Father's watch.

In September of 1950 my parents enrolled me at Yeshiva University High School and Hebrew Teachers Institute. Our years of wandering finally ended. And with hearts full of painful memories, we began a new life in a new country with hard work and high hopes for a brighter future.

I told the story of my survival to show the depths to which human spirits can sink, how a human being can bear torment and unspeakable hardships. It was not meant to distress you, but rather to show you that you should never give up hope. You should always strive for a new dawn while remembering the past and taking strength from it.

My mother, Rebecca.

My parents, Rebecca and Solomon Bichler.

Sitting, left to right: Aunt Doba, my mother holding me, my father holding Beatrice, and Aunt Sarah. Standing, left to right: Uncle Kalman, Aunt Munya, Aunt Mindle, and Uncle Isaac. All except my parents, my sister, and I perished in the Holocaust.

My great grandfather, Zayde Levy.

My grandfather, Yitzhak Kurtzwald, pre-WWII.

My grandmother, Shifra (1947).

My sister, Beatrice, and I in 1939.

My uncles, Isaac and Yeshayahu. Uncle Isaac, pictured on the left, perished in the Holocaust.

My aunt, Munya, and uncle, Samuel. Both perished in the Holocaust, along with their children.

My cousin, Tonia, who perished in the Holocaust.

My great-uncle, Chaim Brenner, with Cousin Benny in 1938.

My sister's class in Krylov.

My cousin, Yehoshua Brenner.

My cousin, Reizel Bichler. She later perished in the Holocaust.

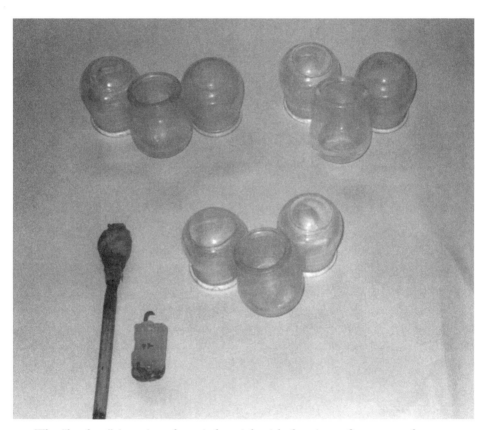

The "bankes," (cupping glasses) the stick with the piece of cotton, and a candle for lighting the stick.

My Aunt Faige, Uncle Yeshayahu's wife. She died in Turkistan in 1942.

My Aunt Rivka, Uncle Yeshayahu's second wife.

Children and counselors of the kibbutz. I am the blond boy in the center, next to the counselor Esther. Poland 1945.

Grandmother Shifra, Sister Beatrice, Cousin Chaya, Sister Iris (Chaya) and I at the DP Camp in Leipheim, 1946.

The public kitchen staff in Leipheim. Top right: my father. Bottom left: my uncle.

My mother, my sister Beatrice, and my cousin Zalman from Pritzk walking in Leipheim, 1947. Zalman was the only survivor from his entire family of Pritzk.

With friends outside the kibbutz in Leipheim. I am at the top left.

My school class in Leipheim entering an assembly hall. I am in the second row, third from right.

A group of children from the kibbutz with Counselor Lopek in Leipheim. I am standing second from left.

This picture was taken outside Barrack 9, which served as our kibbutz in Leipheim. I am on the far left, the only boy in the photo.

My mother holding my sister Iris (Chaya) during a demonstration in Leipheim (DP Camp) for an independent Jewish state.

1946 school outing in Bavaria near the Austrian border. I am seated in the front, fourth from the left.

1947 school outing to Etal outside Garmisch Partenkirchen.

My sister, Beatrice, and Chayim Kochol in a school play in DP Camp.

A ceremony in DP Camp. My sister, Beatrice, is to the left of the camp director.

Girls from the kibbutz on the street of DP Camp in Leipheim. My sister, Beatrice, is third from the left.

Rabbi Eliezer Kagel, principal of the Talmud Torah in the DP Camp in
Leipheim.